THE ROTATING SPAGHETTI FORK
AND OTHER ITEMS YOU CAN'T LIVE WITHOUT

by Cris Cristofaro and Joanna Cotler

A Perigee Book

Perigee Books
are published by
The Putnam Publishing Group
200 Madison Avenue
New York, NY 10016

Book design by Martha E. Sedgwick

Please order carefully. Neither the authors, the publishers, nor the companies represented in this catalog can take responsibility for misplaced orders. All items may be discontinued at the sole discretion of the companies and prices are subject to change.

Library of Congress Cataloging in Publication Data

Cristofaro, Cris.
   The rotating spaghetti fork and other items you
can't live without.

   1. Catalogs, Commercial. 2. Novelties.
I. Cotler, Joanna. II. Title.
HF5861.C74   1985   381'.4567'029473   84-25550
ISBN 0-399-51127-X

Printed in the United States of America
1 2 3 4 5 6 7 8 9 10

Joanna Cotler and Cris Cristofaro are human beings who live on the planet Earth. They see themselves as the torchbearers of the weird, wonderful and wacky world of the American entrepreneur.

2264655

Acknowledgments

NEWS FLASH: MEMPHIS PSYCHIC, VEENA OAKS, PREDICTS FORK FETISHISM WILL FLOURISH IN THIS CENTURY. Said Miss Oaks, "It will come about in the form of a book but only with the generous help of the following people, whose names appeared in my tea leaves: Martha E. Sedgwick, Fred Hodara, Bob Perry, Susanne Jaffe, Sydney Klevatt, Betty Donerson, Robert Edmund, Andrew Christie, Richard Curtis, Linda Emilson, Richard Epstein, Marie Furno Hart, Terre Lantzy, Bruce Lindeke, A. Jerry Luebbers, John Meier, David Mercer, Roger Scholl, and Ruth Van Gordon. I predict there will be much laughter and giggling, also much support and love from family and friends of the authors. My predictions always come true."

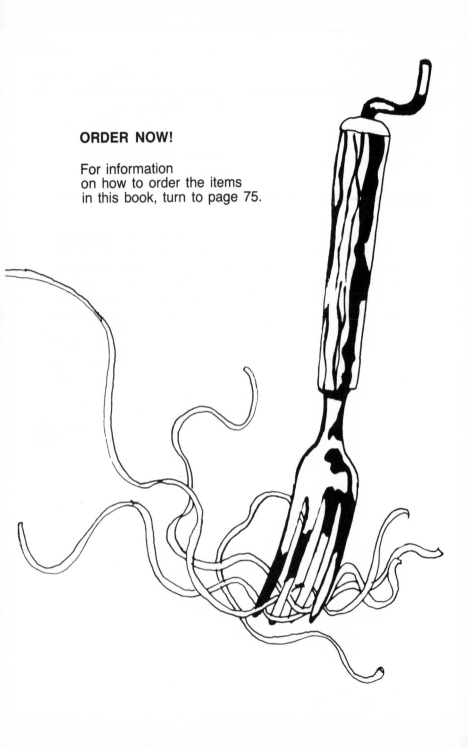

ORDER NOW!

For information
on how to order the items
in this book, turn to page 75.

Introduction

THE ROTATING SPAGHETTI FORK AND OTHER ITEMS YOU CAN'T LIVE WITHOUT is a real mail order catalog of unusual, funny, useful, crazy, and original things culled from the wonderful mail order catalog companies across this country. You can actually order any item that appears in this book because, believe it or not, these things actually exist! We think of this book as a celebration of the joys of mail ordering, a salute to the longevity and ingenuity of American entrepreneurialism. The items we have selected for the catalog don't just make our lives better—they make them funnier, too. They reflect and tell stories about who we are and what we think, the way we see and what we feel—items we take delight in, laugh over, and most important of all, simply *can't live without.* Two thousand years from now when archeologists in what was once America unearth a Car John or a Sunbrella Hat, well, what do *you* think they will say about who we were . . . ?

SUNBRELLA HAT shades you on the go; frees hands for action! Great idea come rain or shine. Wear it anywhere! Headband fits all. Colorful nylon with umbrella action metal ribs. 23″ when open.
SUNBRELLA HAT (OLD VILLAGE, Z460204) **$3.88**

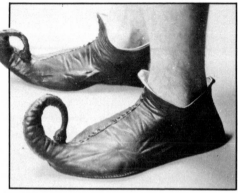

LEPRECHAUN SHOES ... A FASHION MUST! They're huge and green and perfect for any occasion. Complete *your* wardrobe with shoes handcrafted by elves while singing "The Rose of Tralee." Fits all adult sizes. Waterproof poly.
LEPRECHAUN SHOES (OLD VILLAGE, Z547745).................... **pair $8.99**

SOUND ATTACHE CASE. You'll be sure to get the attention you deserve on that crucial job interview if you *sing* your credentials loud and clear through this public-address-system-in-a-briefcase. Everything stores inside the lightweight attache case. Powered by eight "C" cell batteries or AC power pack (included). Quality high fidelity speaker; 5m range microphone. FCC approved. Sets up in seconds. Black vinyl case with gold tone clasps. We guarantee you'll have the only singing resume; be known as the minstrel of the job hunt circuit. And with the handy FM radio built into the case you'll add "pop" to your presentation ("A little light music, sir?").
SOUND ATTACHE (EDMUND SCIENTIFIC, 8408 34 038)
....**$129.00**

JUMBO PEANUT ... Listed in the *Guinness Book of World Records,* this Goliath of the peanut patch is a giant in horticultural achievement, with huge crops of super-size, super-flavor, super-easy shelling peanuts. Plant them, grow them! Then when you hear someone say, "Does he have big nuts!" you'll know they'll mean you. If Carter had had these nuts, he'd still be President.
JUMBO PEANUT (LAKELAND, Z001453H)
...................................**$1.98**

IT'S CAR JOHN TO THE RESCUE! Use it when you're stuck in traffic and rest areas are too far away. Relieves more than tension. Just whip it out; eliminates frequent roadside stops. Styrene rubber, 16-oz. poly reservoir.
CAR JOHN (OLD VILLAGE, Z406090)
...............................**$3.88**

HIDE-A-VAULT. A Letter to our Son, Johnny: "DO NOT OPEN TILL AFTER NUCLEAR HOLOCAUST. Dear Johnny, If you can read this then you'll have lived through the war and be on your own. Go dig under the old willow tree until your shovel hits the Hide-A-Vault, an air-tight, corrosion-proof time capsule, 6″ × 12″, in which we have packed some things you'll need: Mom's recipe for your favorite Moo Goo Gai Pan, the Liberace *Big Note Songbook,* a pair of clean socks and underwear, and one peanut butter and jelly sandwich (made with Wonder Bread to ensure freshness). You'll be OK Love Mom & Pops. P.S. Remember to chew before swallowing." Hide-A-Vault, for your valuables—only you'll know where it's buried!
HIDE-A-VAULT (KRUPP'S, HOVAULT)
...................................**$36.95**

URINAL BAR ACCENT. If you're like us, you'll love snacking out of this urinal-shaped plastic nut and candy holder. Even has "drainholes" at the bottom. Just attach to wall and invite guests to dig in. Approx. 21″ tall × 10½″ wide.
URINAL BAR ACCENT (HANOVER HOUSE, Z571083) **$5.99**

THIS COULD BE YOURS!

INSPECT EVERY SPOT IN YOUR MOUTH WITH ORAVIEW. Explore the uncharted terrain of the orifice so crucial to your well being: your own mouth. Because of its unique tilted and revolving mouth mirror, and light and concave magnifying hand mirror, you can enjoy the miracle of tooth decay, watch plaque, gum disease, and tartar grow before your very eyes! And even see your own uvula! Be your own dentist with Oraview. Not included: wrench, chain saw, sand blaster or acetylene torch. Included: 2 "AA" batteries. 9″ high. 2½″ dia. mirror.
ORAVIEW (EDMUND SCIENTIFIC,......
8408 33 195) **$14.95**

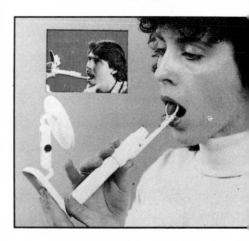

HOME ON THE RANGE. "Hey pardner, set up the 2000-degree furnace and cook us up some pork 'n' beans right in the can! All you need is scrap parts and my Fresnel lens. At 11¾″ square, ¹⁄₁₆″ thick, and with an 8½″ f.l., it gets hot enough to melt asphalt. Let's heat up some of them croissants too."
LENS (EDMUND SCIENTIFIC, 8408 70533) **$14.95**

SINUS HEAT MASK. "Dear Evelyn: The enclosed snapshot is me wearing the Sinus Heat Mask that you so kindly sent. Its pretty printed cotton cover reminds me of that moo-moo you love so much. And thanks to you, my sinus pain, nasal congestion, headaches, allergies, head colds, and tension have all been relieved. You're right, the 6' cord with three settings is really convenient. The 13″ × 7¾″ size adjusts to fit every head in *our* house. Used moist or dry, I wear it every day! Yours always, Fran."

SINUS HEAT MASK (MATURE WISDOM, Z750687)............................$19.95

PLAQUERED KIDNEY. Larger than life and shaped like a rather well-known bean, or a modern swimming pool, this cutaway hand-painted model of a kidney is mounted on a plastic plaque 8½″ × 12″ × 3″ thick. Makes a lovely kitchen accessory, spectacular in rec rooms or hung over your bar. Instructional, too.

KIDNEY MODEL (JERRYCO, J-5033-1)...........$20.00 (3.0 lbs.)

GOOD HELP IS SO HARD TO FIND NOW-ADAYS. Not with RoButler—he's always at your beck and call. No sick days, no salary, no complaints! The first affordable home butler will serve your guests dressed in style (he even comes with black bow tie). RoButler is controlled by wireless hand-held remote control transmitter. Sturdy tray has traction-tread wheels that run on smooth surfaces and low-pile carpet, both indoors and out. Goes forward and back, turns and stops. 11″ × 15″ acrylic tray. Operates on one 9-volt and four "D" cell batteries (not incl.). "Oh, Robutsky, be a sweet little robot and bring me my brew and pretzels."

ROBUTLER (EDMUND SCIENTIFIC, 8408 34 218).........................$49.95

PERSONALIZED LUNCH BAGS. There's nothing worse than opening up your lunch bag to find your son Johnny's sardine and cream cheese sandwich and a pork rind treat, when you'd been looking forward to your very favorite, peanut butter and mayonnaise with a side of boiled okra. Do what Chris, Larry, and Linda did: get Personalized Lunch Bags for the whole family and no more sack mix-ups! 10¾" × 5¼". Specify name (up to 11 letters). 50 paper bags.
PERSONALIZED LUNCH BAGS (BOLIND, D2105)
.... $11.95

"I LOVE YOU" PENNY. Show her how much you care—with this genuine mint condition penny with those all-important words "I Love You" engraved in a heart on its face. A uniquely memorable gift. Show someone special you have sense in love.
LOVE PENNY (JOHNSON-SMITH, 5998).....
.... $0.80 each; 3/$2.15

ICE CREAM PRESS—FOR THE MEAN MOM IN YOU! Now you can create your own ice cream cookie sandwiches for the kids. Pack 'em for their school lunches for a soggy surprise, pop 'em under their pillows for a sticky bedtime treat! Fun and easy and dishwasher-safe, plastic.
ICE CREAM PRESS (HANOVER HOUSE, Z571075) $1.49

FOR THE UPWARDLY MOBILE MR. FIX-IT! A FOUNTAIN PEN TOOL KIT JUST FOR YOU! Don't flash your tools . . . look like an executive and screw at the same time with 1 Phillips, 2 screwdriver heads, an awl, and a screw starter. It's 4⅝" overall, so you can clip it to the pocket of your pin-striped suit. Remember to dress for success by carrying this kit without the tool chest.
PEN TOOL KIT (HANOVER HOUSE, Z531301)
.... $1.59

HOT SEAT!

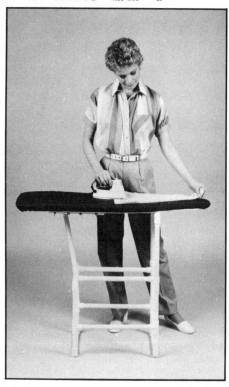

How many times have you asked yourself . . . "Gee, why can't my ironing board turn into a chair?" Presto! The chair that irons out the wrinkles. But careful, gals, don't scorch those buns! Made of heavy-duty P.V.C., your designer ironing board is light and easy to handle. 43″ × 13½″ overall with wooden seat board, ½″ foam pad, and canvas duck cover.
IRONING BOARD/CHAIR (ADAM YORK, Z912873) $49.95

SUN DOTS STOP GLARE. While driving, a mother of six found that when a sesame seed hamburger bun came flying from the back-seat, landing with a THWACK on the windshield, it actually helped stop the glare of the sun. Like most good moms, she turned a rather sticky situation to good use by inventing these sun dots. These filters may be moved readily (un-like hamburger buns) on wind-shield or windows. Cling instantly to glass. Effective in areas visors cannot cover. Package of 3.
SUN DOTS STOP GLARE (BOLIND, 1384) . . . . $3.93; 2/$7.50

SOLAR POWERED PROPELLER BEANIE.
Be the hippest hardhat on the construction site with this bright yellow plastic hardhat—the world's most technologically advanced solar beanie! Its 2″ dia. cell powers the electric motor to speedily spin the 5″ propeller when hat is worn in sunlight. It could propel you to work hard and keep your head awhirl—especially on a clear day on the 95th girder.
SOLAR POWERED PROPELLER BEANIE (JOHNSON-SMITH, 6252)........ $17.98

DON'T JUST STARE AT THE CEILING! NEVER RAISE YOUR HEAD AGAIN! With this amazing TV Bed Viewer eliminate the need to stand or even sit again. Just lay back, place over eyes, and enjoy the scene. Presto! Lightweight, comfortable, and attractive. Glass and plastic, 6″ wide.
TV BED VIEWER (OLD VILLAGE, Z555268)......................... $4.88

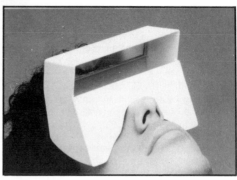

COVERT IS BETTER THAN OVERT. Why use your fists when you can use your wits with this no-nonsense book, *How to Get Anything on Anybody.* It's the A-to-Z guide to undercover operations. Learn how to track anyone . . . anywhere . . . anytime. Organize an intelligence campaign against any target. Scramble a phone conversation or check a driver's record. 268-page paperback.
HOW TO GET ANYTHING ON ANYBODY (EDMUND SCIENTIFIC, 8408 9664) $34.95

NOW A PAINLESS WAY TO CLIP HAIR FROM NOSE, EARS! Precision clippers work with an easy squeeze of handles to snip off long, unsightly nasal hairs . . . No painful pulling. Great for you guys and gals with those bushy ears. Outer shield guards rotary edge. So reach for those hard-to-get spots! 2″ long.
SAFETY NOSE CLIPPER (HANOVER HOUSE, Z559302). $2.99

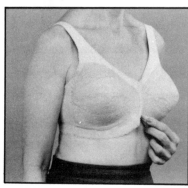

BIG BEAUTIFUL BRA. Stop right here! Been hassled by the police lately for pectoral prominence, or obstructing traffic? Well, we're here to help you with the biggest bra idea in mammary. Featuring sizes up to 50D (!), this bra supports without underwire (!); a foam band crosses under and over to separate, divide, and conquer. No more need for those pesky WIDE LOAD signs.
BRA (HANOVER HOUSE) BACK HOOK (Z751966B); FRONT HOOK (Z751974B) . . . .
$12.77 each; 2/$24.00

ORDER BY MAIL

FUR COAT. Here is canine celeb, Marco Froth, descending from his limo on the way to the premiere of his latest flick, *Dogs Without Women.* Froth's man-made mink fur coat took center stage: fully lined with large ample collar and hooks in back, it is snug, flashy, fitted, and fantastic. Great for your celeb dog, too. Washable; 10 through 16; *personalized.*
FUR COAT (GEORGE'S, 1014). $45.00

ENCOUNTERBATS™. There's nothing better than a good brawl—what better way to say you care? And fighting is *still* OK with these EncounterBats™. Used from preschools to penitentiaries, they're safe, make a loud WHOMPING noise when hit, and aid in anger release. Sturdy and made of foam material, each EncounterBat™ is covered with heavy-duty cloth to give you long, trouble-free use. Great for assertiveness training. Caution: Avoid hitting head, breast, boss, crotch, landlord, or other delicate areas. Comes with cautionary instruction sheet.

ENCOUNTERBAT™ **FOAM BATS (UNIQUITY, A07-00)** . . . . **$48.95 per pair**

CRAZY CRANIUMS

Why not let your hat express the true craziness that goes on inside *your* head with these Crazy Craniums? Whether you're a peabrain, an egghead, or have rocks in your head, be yourself, knucklehead, and order today! Made of hand-painted latex rubber with comfortable foam rubber inserts. Adjustable.

PEABRAIN   (JOHNSON-SMITH, 4987M)
ROCKHEAD   (4908M)
KNUCKLEHEAD   (4985M)
EGGHEAD   (4909M)
. . . . **$9.98 each**

WHAT'S LONG AND GREEN AND FUN TO EAT?

A Yard Long Bean, dummy. That's right, this amazing wonder bean grows a full 3′ long—one bean feeds the whole family! These exceptionally fine-flavored beans are slender, oh-so tender, and full of juicy, pleasing snap-bean taste. Vines grow like mad with bumper crops. Seeds mature in 70 days. Where have you been, wonder bean?

YARD LONG BEANS (LAKELAND, Z003715H)
. . . . 1 pkt/$1.77; 2 pkts/$3.49; 4 pkts/$5.99

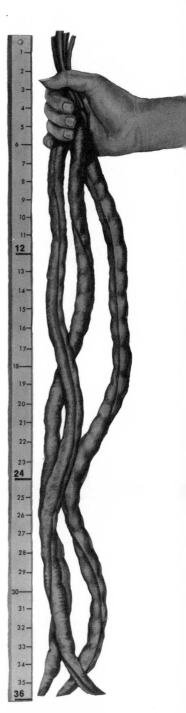

THE CHICKEN THAT LAUNCHED A THOUSAND LAUGHS. The gift of a full-size, realistically colored, 22″ plucked chicken is always a sign of good taste. Can be used in home, office, or school. Doesn't cluck but sure is plucked. Almost finger-lickin' good, but a bit rubbery.

GAG CHICKEN (JOHNSON-SMITH, 3045) $6.98

LE BRIEF SAFARI. Be it out in the jungle where the apes are calling, or in the heart of the city where the subways roar—you should always be suitably clad in le brief underwear and sensible shoes. Not a seam is seen; light stretch nylon with front panel has highcut French styling and a slim sculptured back strap. Brings out the animal in you. In zebra, tiger, or leopard print. Sizes S (28″–32″) and M (34″–38″). Growl.
LE BRIEF SAFARI (NIGHT 'N DAY INTIMATES, Z977173B).................$8.00

$AMAZING PRICES!$

TELL RODENTS, BATS, COCKROACHES TO BUG OFF ... WITH VERMINEX ... A Battery-Powered Ultrasonic Pest Repeller. Delivers an incredible 122 dB of complex sound pressure while using no more than a transistor radio. Enough sound pressure to rid 2500 sq. ft. of creepy, crawly vermin sensitive to ultrasonic waves. Battery-powered, it can be put in unwired storerooms, pantries, cellars, recreatonal vehicles, etc. Uses one 9-volt battery (not incl.). AC adapter is included. 4″ × 2½″ × 1½″, weighs 1 lb.
VERMINEX (EDMUND SCIENTIFIC,.........8408 33 610) $39.95

NAIL DRYER TO THE RESCUE. Stop blowing yourself red-faced! Dry and fly with this baby! Dries nails in two-thirds the normal time. Rest fingers on pressure-sensitive pad. Uses 9V battery, not included. Constructed of sturdy plastic. Nail drying has never been so easy. 4½″ × 7″.
NAIL DRYER (PENNSYLVANIA STATION, Z789040)........................$15.00

HAUTE CUISINE CANAPE MAKER. "Stephanie, darling, you *must* give me your recipe for this delicious canape. What ever is in this decorative multi-colored column of food?" Don't tell, Steph! Made with her own haute cuisine canape-maker, Stephanie concocted these tongue-head-cheese-and-baloney-on-white bread canapes because she loved them so much. Just plunge and pop into mouth. Makes professional-looking hors d'oeuvres. Just press onto anything, then push down plunger for perfectly formed appetizers. Complete with 4 canape cutter shapes, storage case, and 23-page recipe book. **CANAPE MAKER (COLONIAL GARDEN KITCHENS, 3-8936)** $11.75

ADOPT-A-FLEECE! The A.S. Fleece C.A. is calling on all responsible human beings to adopt a Fleece. There are hundreds of homeless Fleeces roaming the countryside in search of a loving home. Fleeces are soft, safe, warm, and friendly. Hold one up to your ear and squeeze—it makes such a sweet sound, like someone walking through snow. *You* can become a foster Fleece Ball parent today for only $4.50—less than the cost of a lousy movie. How can you say no to these 4"-diameter balls of virgin orlon fibers? We've adopted three: Flora, Folonari, and Fluffy Fleece.
FLEECE BALL (UNIQUITY, BB11-00) $4.50

LADYBUGS TO THE RESCUE! This biologically safe army used by government and large growers can be called on to destroy aphids, inchworms, Japanese beetles, mites, muggers, unwanted company, bill collectors. Use for exotic centerpiece, or as living-room wallpaper. About 9000 bugs to the pint.
LADYBUGS (½ pint, LAKELAND, Z000455E)
.... $6.99
LADYBUGS (1 pint, Z000463E)....... $13.50

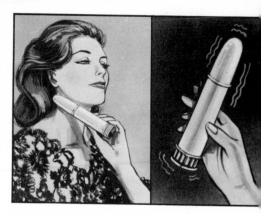

HANDY CORDLESS MASSAGER. Enjoy a tingling, relaxing feeling! Contoured to soothe, tingle, stimulate, excite hard-to-reach areas. It's so easy, no cord or cranking.
MASSAGER (OLD VILLAGE, 7″ Z350512)................. $3.99
(10″ Z350520)................ $5.99
(12″ Z401935)................ $6.99

BAG-O-DOG? No, its Pet-Sac, a versatile sleeping bag for your dog. Does your dog have trouble sleeping on camping trips? Just zip bag open, pop in pooch, and presto—one warm and toasty hound. Machine washable (remove dog before washing), cotton lined with DuPont Hollofil 808 insulation, assorted prints. 30″ × 24″ closed.
SLEEPING BAG (GEORGE'S, 3014)
.... $17.50

THANK GOODNESS! A CARROT CUTTER! Here's an item that could change your life! A cutter specially designed for those tough-to-cut veggies that roll when you slice them lengthwise. Press down and presto—carrot sticks! Terrific time-saver. Sturdy cast aluminum frame, stainless steel blades, cordless.
CARROT STICK MAKER (HANOVER HOUSE, Z559203) $2.99

HAND SIZE MAY VARY.

COVER-UPS FOR BURNERS. Could a paleontologist unearth treasures from the goop that you have accumulated on *your* burners over the years? If the answer is yes, we've got the solution for you! Rid your stove of those fossilized egg remains the old-fashioned way: by hiding them. These neat 'n' nifty cover-ups for burners are sealed acrylic-coated, fit over elements. Set of 4; specify White, Harvest Gold, Avocado. Regular: 1 large, 3 small; deluxe: 2 large, 2 small.
COVER-UPS FOR BURNERS.............
(MATURE WISDOM, Reg. Z480590B; Del. Z480632B).................Each set $7.77

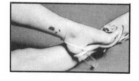

TATTOOS FOR EVERYBODY. Are you one of those "Plain Jane" girls who deep down always wanted to have a tattoo? Well, even if you didn't, now you can with these temporary tattoos. Place them on your ankle, neck, or under your eye. Apply easily with water, will stay on until removed with cold cream. 50 tattoos: flowers, hearts, butterflies, etc. Approx. ½" to 1½".
TATTOOS FOR EVERYBODY (BOLIND, 3060) $7.50

BORED WITH YOUR APPEARANCE? CHANGE THE WAY YOU LOOK AND FEEL WITH ALIEN EARS! Can't afford a new dress, shoes, or earrings? Want to make a fashion statement that will make a unique yet affordable difference? Try these giant pointed ears. Realistically colored; about 4" long.
ALIEN EARS (JOHNSON-SMITH, 4713)...........$2.98

DOES IT SOUND LIKE YOU'RE WEARING TAP SHOES WHEN YOU WALK BAREFOOT? Feel that a chain saw wouldn't be an extreme measure in taking care of your rough, dry, callused foot problems? Why not try this electric callus remover for silky smooth skin on feet, knees, elbows—quickly, safely, gently.
CALLUS REMOVER (HANOVER HOUSE, Z336560).............. $7.99; 2/$13.00
REFILL DISKS (Z336552)...............
..........pkg. of 7/$1.59; 2 pkgs./$1.99

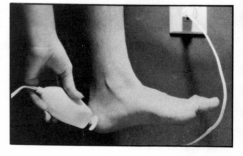

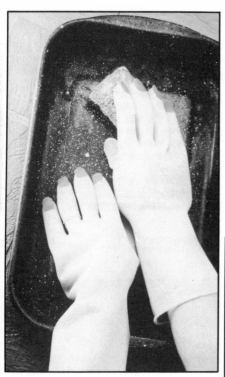

GLAMOUR GLOVES. How do movie stars keep their dishpan hands picture perfect? We asked celebrity Joan Evans: "With Glamour Gloves, darling, I simply adore scouring those grease-caked pans! The red 'fingernails' and pretend diamond ring really make me feel as glamourous as I am. And with Glamour Gloves even *guests* will want to help out." One size fits all.
GLAMOUR GLOVES (COLONIAL GARDEN KITCHENS, 3-5428) $5.95

PROTECT DRESSY BOOTS. Fashion. It's a way of life. Step out on the town with full confidence when you slip your best shoes into these glamourous high-heeled rain boots made from sturdy vinyl. Transparent enough to show off your fine taste in footwear. Wear around the house to coordinate with plastic furniture covers.
PROTECT DRESSY BOOTS (OLD VILLAGE, Z550764) $4.88

SOLAR POWERED VISOR RADIO. A head is a terrible thing to waste—on a hat. You can have *so* much more with this good-looking, lightweight, solar powered AM radio visor. Derives power from the sun or incandescent light source. Good quality sound. Uses standard battery on cloudy day. Fully adjustable cap and headphones. Not recommended for cave dwellers.
SOLAR RADIO VISOR (JOHNSON-SMITH, 4787M) $14.98

21

MOHAWK & PUNK WIGS. Don't you love these flesh colored rubber and synthetic hair wigs? Photographed at their chic Beverly Hills salon, twin hair stylists Mr. Buford and Mr. Barlowe show how every person—from accountant to zoologist—can wear these unique wigs. "No matter who you are, what you do, or how unmanageable your mane!"

MOHAWK WIG (JOHNSON-SMITH, 4015M)...................... **$8.98**
MULTI-COLORED PUNK WIG (4079M)
.... **$8.98**

MAKE YOUR HAND A TABLE. Eliminate the need for table setting, tablecloths, or even tables! With plate clip drink holders, make your guests stand. Clip onto dinner plate rims and safely hold most stemmed and bowl-shaped glasses. Unbreakable, dishwasher-safe plastic; no-slip rubber grip.

PLATE CLIP DRINK HOLDER (RAINBOW OF GIFTS, Z715250)...........
.... **$9.99 set of 12**

EDGAR BERGEN'S INSTANT VENTRILOQUISM RECORD. 12″ long-playing record with comments by Edgar Bergen, Charlie McCarthy, and Mortimer Snerd. Learn ventriloquism fast and easy. Full 44-minute listening time. With these professional instructions you can make your voice come from socks, a pair of plyers—or even make an English muffin talk. Or be more traditional and use a dummy. We're sure you know a few.

VENTRILOQUISM RECORD (JOHNSON-SMITH, 6285) **$7.98**

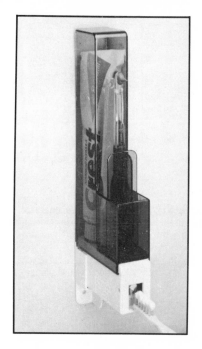

DENTO-MATIC. Are your fingers exhausted from squeezing that toothpaste tube? Have you had enough of that trying, emotional, yet all too necessary daily function? Stylish and economical, this dento-matic dispenses toothpaste automatically; holds toothpaste tube and 4 toothbrushes in a neat, orderly, clean manner. Ivory/smoke plastic unit comes with 1-yr. manufacturer's warranty. 10¼″ × 4″ × 1½″ overall.
DENTO-MATIC (TAPESTRY, Z912667)....$14.95

$**AMAZING PRICES!**$

WHITE TEETH INSTANTLY. A commentary from French artist Monique Blanche: "Painting is my life, so when my teeth began to turn yellow and puce I decided why not paint them too? It really worked! In minutes Beauty White cosmetic dental enamel dried to a lustrous finish that covered stains on my caps and fillings. Dentist's formula is 100% safe, odorless, tasteless, and lasts 3 to 4 months. I'm starting a new series of pearly white paintings inspired by Beauty White's success entitled *Les Bicuspids Blanches.*"
BEAUTY WHITE (OLD VILLAGE, Z350769) $2.99

THE FLYING BIRD FROM FRANCE. No, he is not made of Brie. Oui, he really flies. No, he does not chirp. Oui, he has a marvelous 16″ wingspan and will fly up to 40′ high and a distance of 150′. His power is supplied by twisting a rubber band; his feathers are made of sun-catching Mylar. Oui, you can adjust for up, down, swooping flight—just like a real bird. While this bird is a fake, its durable polypropylene with a rubber beak lasts longer than the real thing!
FLYING BIRD (EDMUND SCIENTIFIC, 8408 42 720)
....$7.95

23

COMIX PACKS WITH PLENTY OF ACTION. You've heard of things crawling out from under rocks? Well, these original, uncensored comix are from *way* underground. There are plenty of great titles we know you'll love: *Anarchy,* our favorite; *Young Lust;* and the ever-popular *Slow Death.* Each package contains at least 4 comix loaded with lust, sleaze, and commies. This is low, folks, really low. Right up our alley.

DIRTY COMIX (KRUPP'S, KGPAC2)	$11.50
HUMOR COMIX (KGPAC3)	$7.50
DRUG COMIX (KGPAC4)	$8.50
NEWEST COMIX (KGPAC5)	$12.00
NEW SEXY COMIX (KGPAC6)	$11.50

MINI SURVIVAL TOOL. It could save *your* life! How many times have you cried in dismay, "If only I had a mini reamer!" Well, now you'll always have one in your hip pocket, along with a knife, ruler, saw, can opener, screwdriver, wrench, cap lifter, wire stripper, compass, and file! Everything but the kitchen sink! All on one handy miniature multi-use tool; weighs only 1 oz. 1¾" × 2¾" with vinyl case and instructions.
SURVIVAL TOOL (JOHNSON-SMITH, 8110M) $6.98

LIFE! IT'S A MIRACLE! The development of a living thing is a mind-boggling process to behold. The heart begins to beat, the organs pump, the shape changes day by day, the arms and legs grow as the . . . tail begins to disappear? It's amazing . . . it's astounding . . . it's a frog! Yes!—this underwater wonder is a rare South American breed. The kit includes crystal-clear plastic aquarium with green gravel, vitamin-rich growth food, and an illustrated "Frog Fun & Facts" booklet. Also enclosed is a certificate which you send with $1.00 to receive your live tadpole by air mail. (Cannot be shipped to California.)
PET FROG SET (JOHNSON-SMITH, 5002F) $7.98

GRAPES, FRUIT OF THE GODS, come to you at last in a big way with these giant black and blue, early-ripening seedless wonders . . . Great for slicing, dicing, but don't stop there! Look at the size of these monsters. Bowl with them, play basketball with them. Or give these giants the ole one-two step for a truly special-tasting home vintage. WOW, they're big mothers!

VENUS SEEDLESS BLUE GRAPES (LAKELAND, Z180059E). . . . . **Each $5.95;**
. . . . **2/$9.79; 3/$12.89; 4/$14.49; 6/$18.99; 8/$21.99**

BUTTER CHURN. "Oh, Muffin, do we have any butter for my corn?" Why run out to the store for butter when you can churn your own at home? We've lost so much in our modernized, mechanized world. Wouldn't it be nice to hear those ole time sounds of sploshing and thlunking that are the joys of churning your own butter? Why not labor a little? This real butter churn is made from 24 pieces of wood, 22″ × 11½″ at base. "Honey, that butter was delicious—but what took you so long?"

BUTTER CHURN (BOLIND, D3708) **$39.95**

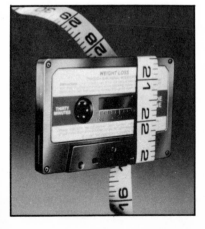

FAT FAT FAT! Aren't you sick of being fat? Try this weight tape—just listen and lose! Pounds! Inches! Rolls! Get rid of that extra flab once and for all. These psychologically designed tapes use subliminal messages with ocean sounds to modify your subconcious and redirect your behavior patterns. Change your state of mind and body and achieve that long awaited goal. "I *won't* eat that second pizza pie . . ."

WEIGHT TAPE (EDMUND SCIENTIFIC, ...
8408 31 537) **$14.95**

MICRO-MINI DICTIONARY. When my friend said to me, "Oh, Dana, you're such a plebian!" I whipped out my World's Smallest Dictionary from my shirt pocket. It contains more than 13,000 words, including those most commonly misunderstood and misspelled. Only 1½″ × 2″ × ¾″, it weighs less than an ounce. Hand-stitched durable vinyl binding protects the fine quality paper. And it's legible! "Plebian," I said. "Yeah, and proud of it!"

MICRO-MINI DICTIONARY (JOHNSON-SMITH, 1600)..................................$4.98

X-RAY GLASSES. "Gee, Penny, what gorgeous hand bones you have." X-Ray Glasses will make you a superman to that special she. It can't be true? Look for yourself! Apparently see bones through skin. Regular size glasses with built-in optical illusion. Amazing and embarrassing. Girls will never trust you again!

X-RAY GLASSES (JOHNSON-SMITH, 3762)
..................................$1.98

PET COOKIE MIX. The smell of apple pie cooling on the windowsill, blueberry muffins warm and screaming for butter, the aroma of nutritional pet cookies turned to a golden brown—this is what being a mom is all about. Wonderful whole grain cookies with no preservatives make great snacks for your favorite pet. 2-lb. bag of cookie mix. Bone-shaped metal cookie cutter (specify large or small). So tasty they disappear before you can say, "No!"

PET COOKIE MIX (GEORGE'S 6010)...................$1.75
COOKIE CUTTER (6011).............................$0.75

WIN $12,000 (OR MORE) WITH THIS MYSTERY TREASURE MAP! No travel or digging required, no diving amongst the sharks, no muss no fuss! Just brains—and this handsome, artistic, U.S. Treasure Map profusely embellished with geographical and historical lore, drawings, clues, rhymes, riddles, etc. for all 50 states. As you solve the many clues you get closer to the final solution and the $12,000 (or more) treasure. Map will tell you how, when, and to whom to write your letter, what the treasure is, and its exact location. A real-life mystery . . . challenge . . . intrigue. And, hey, if you don't win at least the antique appearance of the map makes it suitable for framing. 23″ × 28″.

TREASURE MAP (JOHNSON-SMITH, 147F) ...$4.98

IN CHARTED LANDS. If you're like us, you too must have fond memories of those scientific charts of chick embryos, frog intestines—and our science teacher Miss Herbert's favorite, the earthworm. Return to those thrilling moments in high school science class with these remarkable charts of splayed animals, all explained (?) by a plethora of polysyllabic words of Greek and Latin derivation. Behold once again, in living color, the fish lungs, clam brains, and fern fuzz. How about it, science fans?

SCIENCE CHARTS (JERRYCO, J-2118-1). . . . . **$6.25 each, including postage and handling**
(T-5) EVOLUTION . . . . **(T-15) GRANTIA** . . . . **(T-20) HYDRA** . . . . **(T-30) EARTHWORM** . . . .
(T-35) CRAYFISH . . . . **(T-40) GRASSHOPPER** . . . . . **(T-45) CLAM** . . . . . **(T-55) PERCH** . . . . .
(T-60) FROG . . . . **(T-115) MARCHANITA** . . . . **(T-120) FERN** . . . . **(T-125) PINE** . . . . **RNA** . . . .
DNA . . . . **CHICK EMBRYO**

FOAM ROCKS. They use them in Hollywood, now you can add them to your very own home! These fake stunt rocks are just like the ones so many movie stars have been clobbered with. Foam rubber and grapefruit-sized, these rocks really look like granite. Pretend you're Fred and Wilma Flintstone! Create a disaster in your own home: an avalanche, or Falling Rock Zone. At last an answer to all of your foam rock needs.

FOAM ROCK (JERRYCO, J-1367-1) . . . . **$1.50 (0.1 LBS.)**

PROSPECTING RODS. You've tried to make it on your brains, good looks, charm. And failed. You're *determined* to hit it rich before the age of 20 (or 30, or 40 . . .). When all else fails, try your hand at these imported-from-Europe Prospecting Rods; locate buried treasures and prove yourself the best prospect on your block. Supposedly based on sound scientific facts, we make no claims for success. But we think you'll have fun even if you don't hit the big time (sorry).

PROSPECTING RODS (JOHNSON-SMITH, 4401) **$4.98**

SELECT ANY TUNE ANY TIME ANYWHERE WITH SELECT-A-TENNA. Often wondered what that AM station in Jack Bluff, Texas, is playing? Well, even if you live in Alaska you can tune into stations all across the U.S. with Select-A-Tenna. Turns your radio into a powerful AM receiver! Employs mutually inductive coupling to pull in the weakest stations. Minijack and plug with 50′ of hook-up wire. 10¾″ dia. Hours and hours and miles and miles of enjoyable, down-home, exotic listening!
SELECT-A-TENNA (EDMUND SCIENTIFIC, 8408 72 147) **$39.95**

REARRANGE YOUR FEATURES! Always wanted long fingernails? Ears too small? Nose not big enough? Do you secretly yearn for fangs or bolts in your neck? Well, now's your chance! Spend hours deciding what to wear with these glasses, mustaches, fake eyes, and much more. All pieces are made of non-toxic plastic. With so many choices, who needs cosmetic surgery?
38-PIECE DISGUISE KIT (HANOVER HOUSE, Z567743) **$4.99**

ROCK POLISHING: A BEAUTIFUL HOBBY! Rocks are our friends and if we're nice to them they'll be nice to us. Sure, they don't always look so great, but with a little spit and polish they can be something really special—just like you. This complete kit has all you need to get started: 3-lb.-capacity tumbler with 115V motor and molded rubber barrel; abrasives in coarse, fine, pre-polish and polish; 2 bags of assorted small rocks; jewelry findings (key ring, tie clip). This could be the beginning of a lifetime of rock rapport. 15¾″ × 12½″ × 4⅝″.
ROCK POLISHING KIT (EDMUND SCIENTIFIC, 8408 80 276) **$59.95**

Don't Drink It! Answer It!

It's the real . . . ring. This Coke Bottle Phone is so real-looking it'll make you thirsty. The Touch-tone dialing system is in the base and it features redial and mute keys. For desk or wall use with extra-long cord. FCC approved. 9¾" tall. Calls go better with Coke.

COKE BOTTLE PHONE (OLD VILLAGE, Z568949) $34.99

HEART-Y EGG COOKER. How many times have you said to yourself, "If only my eggs were shaped like hearts"? Give in to that unfulfilled desire. Here's eggs-actly what you need for a heart-y breakfast. Stop yolking around and order one of these Teflon-coated, die-cast, easy-cleaning aluminum pans today. Glass handle cover with metal rim. 7" dia.

**TAKE HEART EGG COOKER.........
(OLD VILLAGE, Z853200) $12.00**

ROCK STAR GLITTER GLOVE. OK. So you don't have four brothers. You haven't had a nose job. You don't date a celeb Princeton coed. You haven't sold more rock albums than anyone else in history. But you *still* can feel like a rock star with this flashy, silvery, flecked, stretch mesh glove on your hand. One size fits all.

**GLITTER GLOVE (JOHNSON-SMITH,.......
Right, 4747M).......................$3.98
GLITTER GLOVE (Left, 4751M)........$3.98
Both for............................$6.98**

THE RISING EXECUTIVE'S POP-UP TIE.
In that financial planning meeting, emphasize your point on rising costs with this pop-up tie. Use any tie—no special tie needed—none supplied. Any place, any time, pops up fast or slow.
POP-UP TIE (JOHNSON-SMITH, 2867)
..................................$3.50

POP-UP TIE

GIANT DAISY BIRD BATH. Blossoms magnificently in your garden! Entice your feathered friends to drink, lounge by the pool, gossip, exchange a few jokes, play a round of mah-jongg, or just relax on the snow-white petals and sunbathe. Made with bright yellow center and green leafy stem, the center of attention, even when it's not in use. Weatherproof plastic and metal. 40″ high.
GIANT DAISY BIRD BATH (MATURE WISDOM, Z338731) $9.99

DE-ODORAMA! Ugh. . . .Does your milk taste of last week's Limburger? Does your butter reek of that hard-boiled egg you lost in the refrigerator last year? Eureka!—a sweet-smelling refrigerator deodorizer to fell those smells. Tests show De-odorama is 8 times as effective as baking soda, 4 times better than activated charcoal. Use in your freezer, too! Reusable after rinsing. Contains natural mineral stones for odor removal.
DE-ODORAMA (MATURE WISDOM, Z563098) $9.95

MAGIC FLOWER CARPET

See Jane. See Jane plant. Plant, Jane, plant. This is the 2-minute way to a season of glorious blooms. Just unroll this weed-resistant carpet of flowers: pre-seeded with over 500 seeds, 6 varieties. Cut Flower Carpet includes snapdragon, zinnia, and other annuals. Lower Border features phlox, petunia, and others. You too will be able to say, "Look, Dick, look!"

FLOWER CARPET (LAKELAND, Tall—Z356915H, Low—Z356923H)................. Each $1.99; .... 2/$3.79; 3/$5.49; 4/$6.95

$AMAZING PRICES!$

ENVIRONMENTS. The sounds of Mother Earth are so beautiful. Now you can cherish them anytime on these records or cassettes. Lean back and relax to *Water Sounds:* ocean waves and distant seagulls, and the gentle lapping of a sleepy lagoon; *Nature Sounds:* melodious bird songs, a rippling stream, a tranquil cricket serenade in an English meadow; *Rain Sounds:* in a pine forest, with a *humdinger* of a roaring, crashing thunderstorm. Great for love, creativity, relief from tension. Records have different effects at different speeds. So listen to Mother . . .

ENVIRONMENTS (JOAN COOK): WATER (LP B466; Cassette B463), NATURE (LP B467; Cassette B464), RAIN (LP B469; Cassette B465)......LP or Cassette $9; .... Any 3 for $25

ELVIS LIVES—ON THESE COLORFUL COLLECTOR'S MUGS! Have a meal fit for the King of Rock & Roll when you sit down to an Elvis-style breakfast: cup o' coffee in your Elvis mug to chase down eight fried eggs over easy, four bowls of home fries, three pounds of bacon, well done, and a bowl of pills. Umm, hummm, what a hound dog. Fun nostalgia for all you Elvis fans!
ELVIS MUGS (HANOVER HOUSE, HOUND DOG Z564690; BLUE HAWAII Z564708; G.I. BLUES Z564716; LAS VEGAS Z564724) .... $7.99 each; 2/$15.00

"**TWINKIES**" **SOAP.** One of America's favorite snack foods is now a soap. Mild yellow soap comes in familiar cellophane wrapper. 4" long. Set of 2. Coming soon: Ketchup Shampoo.
TWINKIES SOAP (JOHNSON-SMITH, 420M) $4.98

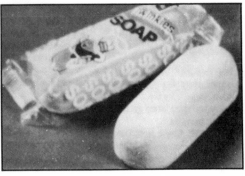

LIFE CAN BE LIKE A MOVIE—WITH YOU THE STAR! The Sound Effects Library adds special effects to your (dull?) life. Perk up a party with "location sounds"; lift your spirits with "mood and emotion effects"; cue in comic or horror title themes when your diet fails (again), or play "impact effects" during a quarrel. Nearly 100 different effects on one LP record will put new life into home video or audio productions too.
SOUND EFFECTS LIBRARY (EDMUND SCIENTIFIC, 8408 34 423) $10.95

IT'S THE GOODY GUMDROP TREE! FUN EATING FOR YOU AND ME! Just load its branches with colorful gumdrops, cheese bits, mini-marshmallows, spam cubes, sardines, etc. Or get a few trees and build yourself a Goody Gumdrop Tree antipasto forest! A party-pretty centerpiece. Plastic. 9½" w. × 12" h. overall.
**GOODY GUMDROP TREE.............
(HANOVER HOUSE, Z509497) $2.99**

ORDER BY MAIL

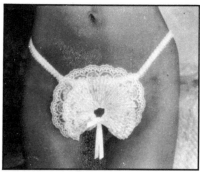

MEOW! Tickle your fancy. Teasingly flirtatious fancy pants of pleated lace and sheer nylon makes this G-string plaque by Jezebel fantastic, and will turn you into the Jezebel of your dreams—and his. It's properly luscious and wild with abandon. White or black; one size fits 4 to 7. (Larger sizes, please order two.)
TEASINGLY PLEASING (NIGHT 'N DAY INTIMATES, Z884098A) $10.00

THE BURGER BANK. Burgers galore with this tray-o-burgers that stacks, shapes, stores, and dispenses burgers like an ice cube tray. There'll be burgers for the whole family, and more: burgers for the Fiftieth Reunion of the United Relish Workers; have Burger Bees; invite your friends over for a Burger Klatch. Just press ground meat into molds, stack next tray on top. Dishwasher safe. (Set of 4 trays.)
POP-IT BURGER (COLONIAL GARDEN KITCHENS, 3-4559) $6.88

THINKING OF GOING INTO POLITICS? It's a tricky business and you'll need all the help you can get. With these extremely realistic full-head rubber or vinyl character masks made by the finest mask makers in the world, at least you'll stand a fighting chance 'cause, hey, you'll be two-faced. But distinctively so. Also great for Halloween or costume parties. Some masks come with synthetic hair, others with skin so real it's hard to tell it's not your own.

CHARACTER MASKS (JOHNSON-SMITH)
REAGAN (#4999)............ $17.98
CLOWN (#4359)............. $19.98
DARTH VADER (#4616)...... $39.98
DIRTY OLD MAN (#4645)..... $17.98

PERSONALIZED ONE DOLLAR BILL. Everyone loves money. Now everyone will love you, with your face printed on one of these personalized one dollar bills. Imagine being tucked in someone's warm pocket all day long, being lovingly handled. Hot stuff, eh? Not hot, real (legal) tender. Send any clear photo (no negatives).

PERSONALIZED ONE DOLLAR BILL (BOLIND, D2016C).................. $9.95
EXTRA COPIES (same photo) (D2016CC)
.... $6.50

BREAK INTO NATIONAL POLITICS with *The Science of Electronic Surveillance.* This book details telephone room eavesdropping devices, general-purpose protection systems, microphones, wire taps, and tape-recording devices. With detailed charts and illustrations. 9″ × 12″. 105 pages. Before attempting the Democratic National Committee Office read this book—or you may be in trouble (again).

THE SCIENCE OF ELECTRONIC SURVEILLANCE (EDMUND SCIENTIFIC, ...
8408 33 578) $34.95

ANTI-MONOPOLY. From our mirror earth, where up is down and down is up, comes Anti-Monopoly, the "Bust the Trust" Game. At last, you who've always lost the game, get to indict that hard-core Boardwalk Monopoly Holder and prove that being a swell person *does* get you ahead in our world, for once. Complete equipment and instructions included.
ANTI-MONOPOLY (JOHNSON-SMITH, 5021H)
.... **$16.98**

MIDGET CAMERA. "Estelle, isn't that Jackie O? And there's a UFO! *Where's* the camera?" Well, Estelle, you'll never miss a snapshot again with this 3½" × 3½" midget camera. Takes 12 beautiful color or black-and-white pictures using 126 Instamatic-type film. Small enough for pocket or purse. Comes with a wrist strap for your convenience. Bright viewfinder. Sturdy construction. No threading.
POCKET CAMERA (JOHNSON-SMITH, 4900M)
.... **$2.25**
Black/White 126 film (4901).............. **$1.98**
Color 126 film (4902)................... **$2.65**

THE BE NOUVEAU RICHE WALL SAFE. So you don't have a pool. A tennis court. A butler. But now you too can feel like a millionaire with this nouveau riche wall safe. You don't have a painting to hide it behind? This safe's ingeniously disguised as an electrical outlet (even the rich have those—they're just by the pool). Features an extra deep storage bin (hole in wall not included). Caution: don't stick your key in the wrong socket—it could prove a hair-raising experience. Ivory styrene; 2⅜" × 7½" × 3⅝"; EZ installation. 2 keys included.
WALL SAFE (OLD VILLAGE, Z518761) **$4.88**

ME-DOLL™. It's the Me-Doll™, a safe, acrylic, distortion-free mirror-faced doll with the perfect image of the face you love most—your own! Cuddly stuffed cloth body comes with colorful removable clothing. Great for language development, socialization skills, emotional growth, and speech reading. Comes complete with teacher's guide. Also makes a great make-up mirror for you moms.
ME-DOLL™ (UNIQUITY): 24" White Skin (AM168-00); 24" Brown (AM169-00) .... **$38.00 each**

THE DWARF BANANA PLANT

(Sing to the tune of "The Girl from Ipanema")

Short and long and yellow and bunchy,
The Dwarf Banana Plant grows on your porch-y,
And when your neighbors pass by they'll ooh and sigh . . .

Tree grows five feet in any dive,
In patio sun it surely will thrive,
So bananafy your home the tropics way.

Oh, you will love it so madly!
Yes, you will give your heart gladly,
For fine bananas so handy
Every day when you sit down to eat—
Bananas fresh picked and so sweet!

Short and long and yellow and bunchy,
The Dwarf Banana Plant grows on your porch-y,
And when your neighbors pass by they'll ooh and sigh . . .
DWARF BANANA PLANT (LAKELAND, Z122101E) . . . .
. . . . **Each $7.99; 2/$14.75; 3/$19.50; 4/$22.50**

GEODESIC DOME KIT. Having trouble finding an apartment? For only $39.95 build your own home—all you'll need is this kit and a parking space or vacant lot. These heavy 16-gauge galvanized steel Star Plates have special channels that grip the framework of moderate-sized buildings and make construction a snap. Choose from a Geodesic dome or a 4 × 4 post construction using the Frame Up kit. Geodesic dome kit lets you bolt together 25 2′ × 2's, 2′ × 3's, or 2′ × 4's which form the skeleton of a variety of structures. Frame Up kit lets you build a variety of 4 × 4 vertical post structures with the 6 connectors included. Just drill holes in the struts and bolt to the Star Plates using ⁵⁄₁₆″ bolts (not incl.). One size fits roof of any domed structure, seals out water.

GEODESIC DOME KIT (EDMUND SCIENTIFIC, 8408 31 947) $39.95
FRAME UP KIT (8408 33 916) $34.95
DOME CAP (8408 33 915) $14.95

WORLD MAP WALLPAPER. Today your wall. Tomorrow the world. Now you can experience the thrill and excitement of being your very own Il Duce with this world map wallpaper. Where will your next incursion be? Your next embargo? Your next invasion? *You* decide! Mural measures 12′ × 9′ wide, can be trimmed to fit most wall space. Heavy stock laquered paper is easy to wipe clean. Installs easily in 8 sections.
WORLD MAP WALLPAPER (RAINBOW OF GIFTS, Z716589) **$44.99**

ALTIMETER. An inquisitive consumer writes: "While watching TV last night my husband, Daryl, asked me, 'Melon Ball (he always calls me that!), what's our present altitude?' I was dumbfounded—and downright stumped." Well, Mrs. Ball, now you can keep this crucial information at your fingertips with this fast, accurate altimeter with readings from 0–15,000′; when bracket is removed fits in your pocket. 3⅜″ dia., self-adhesive base.
ALTIMETER (BOLIND, 687) **$23.95**

FLASH! LARGE FOREIGN POWER'S SECRET ATTEMPT TO LAUNCH OWN MOON ENDS IN THE BAG—OF MOON DUST! This collector's item is now available to the general public at a suspiciously reasonable price. In fact, this reporter has uncovered the hoax that these 1-lb. bags masquerading as "Moon Dust" are really just soil purifier. Once again, world powers play with the wits of the common man.
MOON DUST (JERRYCO, J-2536-1) ...... **$1.25 (1.1 lbs.)**
Ten bags, Ten bucks (J-2536-10) ...... **$10.00 (10.5 lbs.)**

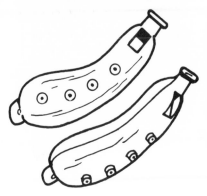

GHERKIN GERSHWIN KIT. Tears will spring to your eyes when you toot "Fascinatin' Rhythms" on your 4-inch, 4-note green pickle whistle. Be the life of the party, or start your own chamber pickle ensemble! Add a dilly of an instrument to your home! Note: A woman loves a man who can play his pickle well.
PICKLE OCTET (JERRYCO, J-2341-8)..........
.... **$2.00 (0.4 lbs.)**
500 WHISTLES (J-2341-500)...$50.00 (18.0 lbs.)
(For a Mormon Tabernacle–size Pickle Choir)

FOLDING STRAW HAT. Gay Paree strikes another blow to the fashion world with this essential fashion accessory. This trés chic hat folds into tiny 6″ roll, so you can slip into pocket or purse. An absolute must for any well-dressed woman on the go. Multicolor woven straw. Opens to 16″ protection from sun's rays.
STRAW HAT (OLD VILLAGE, Z535211)
.... **$3.99**

THE SERENADING SOLAR POWERED KEYCHAIN. Be wooed by the melodic refrain from this serenading solar keychain. Expose this electronic marvel to sun or bright light and it will play "You Are My Sunshine." Sing along even when skies are gray. A great conversation piece to leave your friends speechless. No batteries. And best of all, it has no moving parts to wear out. Solid state music box, sound generator, and speaker along with 4 space-age solar cells are built into this unique, lightweight keychain. Less than 2″ × 3″ and only ¼″ thick!
SOLAR KEYCHAIN (JOHNSON-SMITH, 369M)
.... **$8.98**

INFLATABLE BICYCLE SEAT! A unique slim-line, orally inflatable large wedge-shaped cushion lets you ride in comfort endlessly on your end. Eases soreness from road shocks. Air cushion slips neatly over most 10-speed and standard bicycle seats; raises fanny for a more provocative look.
BICYCLE SEAT (JOHNSON-SMITH, 4799M)......................... **$6.98**

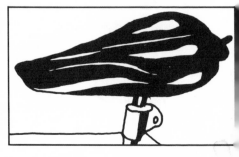

CAUGHT YOUR HEIFER FEEDING ON NAILS AGAIN? NO PROBLEM WITH COW MAGNETS.... Not for attracting cows! Farmers use them to trap metal in the stomachs of their cows—we're sure you'll find them useful too! They are smooth, cylindrical magnets with rounded edges. Each moo-moo magnet measures 3″ long with ½″ dia. Lift capacity of 75 lbs.—in case your cow decides to chew on an anvil. Pkg. of 2.
COW MAGNETS (EDMUND SCIENTIFIC,........ 8408 31 101) **$12.95**

OH, MY GOODNESS, HELEN, COVER YOUR EYES: When your guests ask for drinks on the rocks, you'll really deliver with these sexy stripper glasses. Just add ice and watch them take it off, take it *all* off. *Don't worry,* they'll redress as glass empties. For a quick strip—just a tease—wet outside of glass. Set of four 10½-oz. glasses.
STRIPPER GLASSES (OLD VILLAGE, Z403816—Gal Strippers; Z425025—Guy Strippers) ..... **Set $9.99; Any 2/$18.50**

OPENING HAS NEVER BEEN SO EXCITING! At last, this tab can opener is as handy as your own fingernail—but it *won't* chip or break or look unsightly, thank goodness. Plastic opener lifts up can tabs; magnetic hangup, too. You'll wonder how you ever lived without it.
TAB OPENER (HANOVER HOUSE, A558965) **$1.89**

NO MORE PIZZA FACE! Are you tired of using bobby pins and your sand blaster to remove those unsightly blackheads? Is your face so oily that you're sure it will be declared a National Resource? Sure, hygiene's not *our* bag either, but we highly recommend this remover to aid in the blight of complexion calamities. This scientifically designed pump "lifts" out ugly blackheads gently, safely to achieve clear skin. Makes men more handsome, women more beautiful. Made in U.S.A., naturally.
BLACKHEAD REMOVER (JOHNSON-SMITH, 4641) **$3.50**

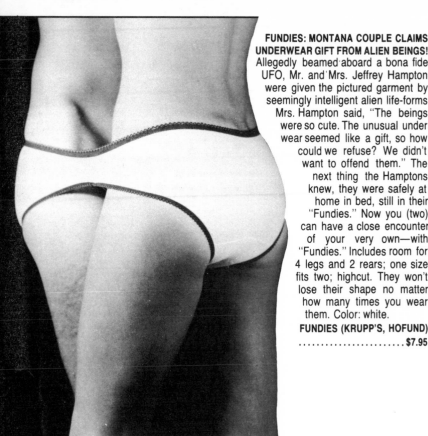

FUNDIES: MONTANA COUPLE CLAIMS UNDERWEAR GIFT FROM ALIEN BEINGS!
Allegedly beamed aboard a bona fide UFO, Mr. and Mrs. Jeffrey Hampton were given the pictured garment by seemingly intelligent alien life-forms. Mrs. Hampton said, "The beings were so cute. The unusual underwear seemed like a gift, so how could we refuse? We didn't want to offend them." The next thing the Hamptons knew, they were safely at home in bed, still in their "Fundies." Now you (two) can have a close encounter of your very own—with "Fundies." Includes room for 4 legs and 2 rears; one size fits two; highcut. They won't lose their shape no matter how many times you wear them. Color: white.
FUNDIES (KRUPP'S, HOFUND)
.... **$7.95**

UNREAL ANTS. The New Wave fashion phenomenon that's infesting the nation! Glue them on your face, put them in your pants. Also suitable for more traditional ant needs such as garnishing your friend's lunch. We guar*ant*ee an *ant*ipasto of good fun. The *ant*ithesis of good taste? Sure, but don't be *ant*ediluvian.
A DOZEN UNREAL ANTS (JERRYCO, J-2399-1) .... **$2.00 (0.1 lbs.)**

GIANT Z-I-P-P-E-R. So you think you have what it takes! For folks of large dimensions (and imaginations) this may be the zipper of your dreams. Yup, 41 big inches long, fellas. Laid flat, it's 1″ wide and is stopped at both ends. Great for giants. Use as a belt or carry one as a spare to impress your dates. Believe it or not, this zipper is *big.*
GIANT ZIPPER (JERRYCO, J-1805-3).... 3 zippers $1.50 (0.2 lbs.)
(J-1805-50)......................... Box of 50 $15.00 (2.6 lbs.)

YARD LONG CUCUMBER. Hey, gals? Where has this cuke been all your life? You'll always have enough with this big guy. Grow it anywhere, for any reason. Makes the world's largest dill; can be grown on ground or trellis for maxi length and straightness. Your neighbors will say, "Have you seen his? I'm green with envy!" Seeds, starter pots, tray, instructions.
YARD LONG CUCUMBERS (LAKELAND, Z008037H) Each $1.79; 2/$3.29; 3/$4.49; 4/$5.29
DELUXE KIT (Z008789H)................. $2.29

41

LAST SUPPER TABLECLOTH

Now you can break bread over this famous da Vinci painting, beautifully reproduced in gold color on heavy-gauge white plastic background. Suppers will last and last with this wipe-clean surface that you can use over and over again. For holidays, also makes an inspirational centerpiece on larger tables. 54″ × 54″.
TABLECLOTH (JOHNSON-SMITH, 4653Y) $3.98

WANT TO WALK ON WATER? No problem!—with these giant inflatable foot shoes. More than 20″ long, these inflatable feet will satisfy any fetish. Super in the water for skiing or floating. Cushions your step and lightens your load. Inflates in a jiffy! Made of durable, flexible plastic.
MONSTER FEET (JOHNSON-SMITH, 3024M)
......................................$3.98

KNEE CUSHIONS TAKE THE ACHE OUT! Thick, sumptuous spongy rubber pads let you kneel on the cold ground for hours. Great for gardeners, floor scrubbers, and the extremely religious. Canvas straps adjust for custom-comfort. Complete with nonslip surface.
KNEE CUSHIONS (MATURE WIDSOM, Z539577) $2.99

ROTATING SPAGHETTI FORK. The pasta fork with a twist! So practical! It really works! Prevents wrist strain from twirling the old-fashioned way. Wind up those noodles more swiftly and accurately with the fork that's got a crank. Magnifico!
SPAGHETTI FORK (JOHNSON-SMITH, 3725)
....$3.50

IT'S A BLOODY MIRACLE! Pictured is an English housewife, displaying giant 16-lb. cabbage. She can hardly lift it! You won't be able to lift *your* vegetables or fruits either after you place these Plant-Growth Pellets near their roots. Great for flowers, too. Be careful, guys, when you lift that tomato tonnage and those humongous heads of lettuce.
MIRACLE PLANT-GROWTH PELLETS (LAKELAND) Standard (160: Z365742H)
.... **$3.49**
Economy (320: Z365759H)........ $6.49

CALVIN SWINE™ BOW TIE. Impossible to find—an honest to goodness pig bow tie. Now you'll be the pig man on campus, thanks to this newest creation by world renowned pig fashion designer Calvin Swine™, who says, "At Pork U., it's all the rage amongst the Yuppies (you know, Young Upwardly Mobile Pigs)." Traditional cut, easy to tie. 100% silk. Subtle Pink Piglets on Navy, Silver on Navy, Silver on Deep Red. Please specify color.
CALVIN SWINE™ BOW TIE (HOG WILD!)
.... $15.00

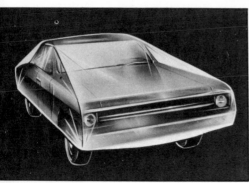

PORTABLE GARAGE. "Okay, Jimmy, you can use the car tonight, as long as you put it in the garage when you get home." "Gee, thanks, Ma. And don't worry—the easy-on, elastic-bottom, tight-fitting, non-cracking-or-peeling garage is already in the pocket of my studded leather chaps."
PORTABLE GARAGE (HANOVER HOUSE) ....
13′ (sports cars, J380808)....... $10.99
16′ (compacts, J380816)......... $11.99
19′ (standards, J380824)......... $13.99
21′ (large cars, J380832)......... $15.99

THE THIRD THUMB™. We're primates. Admit it. But most primates are luckier than we are. It would be nice to be able to eat a can of pork 'n' beans with our feet while swinging from a tree. But, noooo. We homo sapiens have been forced to use our superior intellect to come up with alternative methods for those times when two hands just aren't enough. Hark! The Third Thumb™—the acupressure equivalent of a back scratcher. The Third Thumb™ gives you leverage to reach those parts of your body that are hard to handle with two hands. It's thumb fun! Comes with all-thumbs instruction booklet.
THE THIRD THUMB™ ACUPRESSURE STICK (UNIQUITY, AM252-00) $10.95

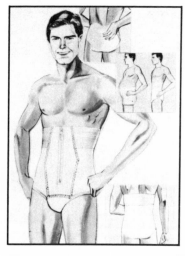

A ROMANTIC INTERLUDE: "Oh, Moose, oh, oh . . . Moose! You're wearing a girdle?" "It's OK, Sandra, it's just my wide-band back supporter, which helps support my lower back while making my waist and hips look inches slimmer. Did I mention it's made of nylon Lycra spandex?"

BACK SUPPORTER (HANOVER HOUSE)
Sm........................ 29–32", Z382176)
Med.................... (33–35½", Z382184)
Lg..................... (36–38½", Z382192)
XL...................... (39–42", Z382200)
XXL..................... (43–48", Z382218)
.... Each $13.44; 2/$26.00

WHAT A TREAT! FEET FOR YOUR MEAT! Now, you can dress your beef in style with these fabulous meat feet. Penny Loafers for your pork? Thongs for your turkey? No!—but feet designed especially for meat that can't be beat for neater roasting. Eliminates messy baked-on oven racks. Feet are dishwasher safe. Can also be used for fruit sculpture, displays—or just use your imagination.
MEAT FEET (HANOVER HOUSE, Z559773)............Pkg. of 3 $2.99

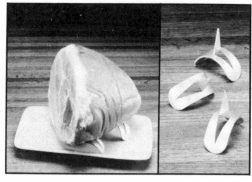

KEYSTONE. Naturally disguised key holders, perfect for country living and city dwellers alike. A secret door and compartment hold up to 4 spare keys. Feel secure in knowing there's always an extra key. So what if yours is the only door in town with a rock sitting outside of it? Might be advisable to glue to ground.
KEYSTONE (OLD VILLAGE, Z709022)
.... $4.88 each; 2/$9.00

45

CHIN STRAPS. As Mother used to say, "You have to suffer to be beautiful." And we should know, shouldn't we, gals? But suffer no more with this featherlike and oh-so-comfortable beauty mask, scientifically designed. Washable, adjust-a-band construction fits snugly, smoothly around chin, jawline, cheeks. Wear as you read, work around the house, or party.
CHIN STRAP BEAUTY MASK..............
(HANOVER HOUSE, Z498725)........$4.99

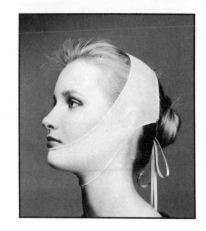

headlights for humans

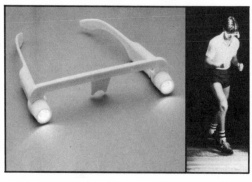

The human species has evolved to a high state—but not so much that we can read in the dark. Now, through the wonders of modern science come headlights for humans, so that you can do just about anything in the dark with both hands free. Designed to be worn like glasses, they're great for night hobbies, jogging, walking, or cycling. Coming soon: tail lights for humans, a safety feature for behind.
HEADLIGHTS (EDMUND SCIENTIFIC, 8408 33 250) **$14.95**

EROTIC AEROBICS ... for sexual fitness. Who needs gravity boots? Boxing bags? Treadmills? Now there's something better: Erotic Aerobics. Zia Odel, that svelte, sexy lady you may have seen on talk shows, has recorded "intimate exercises" on both records and cassettes to get your love life in shape. You'll do it to classical music—using exercises Zia calls "Pelvic Pleasures," "Turn & Tease Me," "Rotations for Arousal," and much, much more. It's a love-toning experience, and a muscle must.
EROTIC AEROBICS (KRUPP'S, Record and Cassette REROBIC) **$9.95**

46

A PACK OF LIES. Over 50 best-loved lies for business and pleasure (including 2 blank cards for personal favorites). Don't waste any more time groping for the right lie—simply pick a card. "This was a special evening for me." "You never got my message?" "Love your dress." And the all-pervasive, "It's in the mail." You need never be at a loss for words again. These lies really work—"We promise!"
A PACK OF LIES (THE FULL DECK) ... $3.50

TOM-PATO KIT!

A GREAT DISCOVERY! Only in the space age can tomatoes flourish above ground while potatoes ripen below. Two for the price of one. Your friends won't believe their eyes! Illustration indicates performance under optimum conditions. Each kit has 6 sets for big crops.
TOM-PATO KIT (LAKELAND, Z101162E) $5.49; 2/$9.79; 3/$12.95; 4/$15.49

THE ROTATING SPAGHETTI FORK AND OTHER ITEMS YOU CAN'T LIVE WITHOUT. A spectacular, one of a kind, real and unusual 80-page mail order catalog of cheap thrills, what nots, why fors, and you'll-need-'ems. Witty and entertaining; great buys! No cord or cranking. Batteries not included (or necessary). Not dishwasher safe. 5¼″ × 8″.

THE ROTATING SPAGHETTI FORK AND OTHER ITEMS YOU CAN'T LIVE WITHOUT Check your local bookstore. . . . . . .
. . . . **$$$ Priceless**

NARCISSISTIC DOG DISH. Originally developed by famous Viennese doggie psychologist, Dr. Heimlich Man-Hoover: ''I have seen much psychological disorder in ze canine community. Anna—oh, vat a deeply troubled husky suffering from anorexia dogosa und a tragic case of bone envy. She overcame her neuroses with ze dish.'' This miraculous dog dish has a 5½″ base diameter with a 4⅜″ mirror glued inside the bottom of the bowl. Will cast a helpful reflection on the narcissistic pooch in your home.
NARCISSISTIC DOG DISH (JERRYCO, J-1797-1) . . . . . $1.25 (0.3 lbs.)

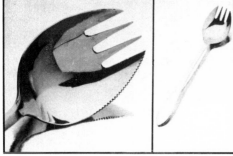

IT'S NOT A SPORK OR A KNOON! IT'S THE UNITENSIL—FORK, KNIFE, AND SPOON ALL IN ONE! Eliminates table clutter and table setting confusion; great for camping. Quality stainless steel made by a precision cutlery company. Specify right or left hand. Set of 4. Coming soon: the Uniscrewtula—corkscrew, meat cleaver, and spatula all in one.
UNITENSIL (HANOVER HOUSE, Z563007) **$3.99**

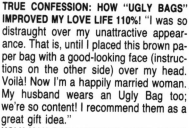

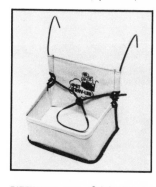

CAR SHADES. Hey, man, even a car needs to be "cool." And yours *can* be, with some shades of its own. Anti-glare and anti-heat, they'll block 70% of the sun's rays. Made of chic see-through vinyl, they work just like ordinary shades, and are held down by a suction cup. So be hip: Make your car feel as cool as you are.
CAR SHADES (MATURE WISDOM, Z48285)
...........................**$7.77; 2/$14.00**

ELECTRIC WINDSHIELD WIPER GLASSES. For showers, hot tubs, executives on the go—these glasses provide clear vision in steamy situations. The flick of a "secret" switch makes these extraordinary specs! Hide standard battery (not incl.) in pocket. Made of sturdy plastic. And, gosh, they're such attractive frames!
WIPER GLASSES (JOHNSON-SMITH, 3190)
....**$9.98**

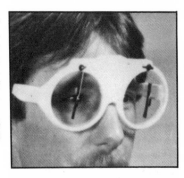

FLASHLIGHT HOLSTER. "Dara, look at *him* —what a stud with that flashlight holster strapped to his belt! It's so handy—keeps his hands free for *me*. Made for durability with a metal stud–reinforced loop. All leather, fits all belts and all guys. Like wow." Flashlight not included.
FLASHLIGHT HOLSTER (JOHNSON-SMITH, 4074).................................**$1.98**

FUZZY DICE . . . with a difference. We admit these have been around forever. And there's a reason. We love 'em, *you* love 'em. Be dicey, and wear them as fashion accents with your mink. Or be traditional, hang on rear view mirror. Or go creative, and enhance your living room decor. Nice to fondle, they're mold-resistant. Available in 2 sizes, though all are white with black dots.
FUZZY DICE (JOHNSON-SMITH) ....
2½″ (3101Y)........................ **$4.98**
4″ (3087Y) **$7.98**

OUR PUPPY'S BABY BOOK. This delightful book has plenty of room for photos, locks of hair, first flea collar. Modeled after a human baby book, it contains sections for Family Tree, First "Accident," First Birthday, Paper Training Day, First Girlfriend, First Christmas, Paw Print, and more. Cloth bound, gold stamped, and printed on special-finish ivory paper, it makes a perfect gift for the proud puppy parent. 32 pages, 9" × 6".
PUPPY'S BABY BOOK (GEORGES, 5001)......
Pink, for girls............................ $5.95
(5002) Blue, for boys.................... $5.95

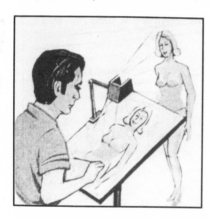

THE ONE-MINUTE ARTIST. Artists make big money. You can too! You don't have any talent? Look in the art galleries—neither do they! At least *you'll* be able to paint or draw recognizable objects, people, or scenes with ease. This Art Reproducer reflects the view in front of you onto paper. Reduce or enlarge, use color or black and white for accurate, proportionally correct "art" in just minutes. No lessons, no talent, no art dealer necessary. Made of plastic, metal slide and stand. About 7" high.
ART REPRODUCER (JOHNSON-SMITH, 6916).............................. $2.98

NUDIST PENS: FOR GUYS AND GALS. Writing is tough—and boring. But it *can* be a rewarding experience with these extraordinary pens. Just turn them over and watch those swimsuits disappear! Aids idea development, creativity (though not concentration). Turn writing into an exciting adventure for you and your fantasies.
NUDE PENS (HANOVER HOUSE, LADY Z533539; MAN Z533547) ..... Each $1.99; any 2 for $3.50

HOT AIR BALLOONS. Got a lot of hot air? Put it to good use by inflating these colorful paper balloons. They can lift anything weighing up to ½ lb. You can send two Quarter Pounders about 200' into space on just hot air! A repair kit is included, containing 10 pre-cut gores, 6' or 14 gauge wire for ring and core. Burgers aloft!
HOT AIR BALLOONS (EDMUND SCIENTIFIC):......
12' (8408 31 333).......................... $14.95
9' (8408 60 691)............................ $8.95
6' (2) (8408 71 866)....................... $12.95

FUR PHONES. Muffs for your lobes that sing! Outer Ear Science has been stumped for decades by the problem of how to keep ears and mind toasty and attentive simultaneously. The answer—ear muff stereo headphones, with high quality speakers, adjustable headband, and 3.5-mm plug which fits into any portable radio or cassette player. No longer will you suffer the effects of Cold Ear Cold Mind Syndrome, no more will you fear Lobe-otomy. A revolution in our era!
FUZZY HEADPHONES (JOHNSON-SMITH, 6023M)
....$14.98

BRAVA FOR THE BRA VAULT. Ladies! This secret pocket hides money, valuables close to your chest. Lets you travel securely in the knowledge that your bank will never go bust. Be discreet when making change. Dainty 4″ × 3″ nylon pouch fastens to bra straps. White only. (Compatible with BIG, BEAUTIFUL BRA, PAGE 13.)
TUCK-AWAY (HANOVER HOUSE, Z339796)
....$1.79

REST STOP FOR HEADS. "Sometimes my feet feel really active but my head needs a rest. That's when I give it a break with my space age headrest made of high density polyethylene and foam, scientifically and orthopedically designed. It makes me feel better in 2 minutes (I have a small head). Normal people will feel body tensions reduced in just 10 minutes. Compact too. So give in to your head—it's the only one you've got!"
SPACE AGE HEADREST (EDMUND SCIENTIFIC, 8408 31 705) $24.95

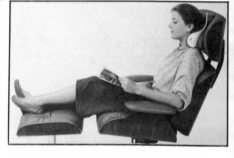

NEED A JOB? Interested in a career as a smuggler? Or as a narc? Here are two books to help you with your education. For the smuggler, *The Complete Book of International Smuggling.* Enjoy plenty of adventure, big salaries, and unheard-of job benefits. For you narcs, on the other hand, there's the *Drug Enforcement Administration Narcotics Investigator's Manual*—all you need to know about informants, entrapment, interrogation, and undercover surveillance. And best of all, plenty of good drugs too.
THE COMPLETE BOOK OF INTERNATIONAL SMUGGLING (KRUPP'S, BKSMUG)..... **$14.95**
D.E.A. NARCOTICS INVESTIGATOR'S MANUAL (BKDEAMAN)..........................**$50.00**

SAVE THE BALES T-SHIRT. Endangered species threatened by Florida Coast Guard. A joint effort is needed. Show your support and voice your objections to this tragic waste by wearing this politically correct T-shirt, silk-screened in full color on bright yellow poly/cotton. Specify size when ordering: S–M–L–XL.
SAVE THE BALES T-SHIRT (KRUPP'S, TSR68) $9.95

WORLD'S SMALLEST HARMONICA. Be the life of Cell Block B with the world's smallest harmonica! Easy to smuggle into jail 'cause it's only 1⅜" long, yet its reeds provide a perfectly tuned, full diatonic octave. Very handsomely made by Hohner, with 4 single holes, 8 reeds. Key: C. With key chain. So serenade your cellmates as they're marched to solitary. Caution: Do not take internally.
WORLD'S SMALLEST HARMONICA (JOHNSON-SMITH, 4210) $4.98

TABBY TOILET TRAINER. Tired of nose clips, oxygen tank, and polyethylene gloves when cleaning your cat's box? Kitty litter problems are no fun. Train your cat to use the toilet! Kit contains a unique vinyl form which fits under the toilet seat during training. Special herbs and complete instructions will have your puss using the toilet just like you.
TABBY TOILET TRAINER (KRUPP'S, KTTT)
. . . . $3.98

53

SHOW BUT DON'T TELL! Remember stuffing socks under your blouse? Remember padded bras? Burn all that stuff! These silicone breast forms fill out today's active women's clothing without unsightly bumps or ridges. Natural weight and feel. Non-irritating, not affected by salt water, chlorine, or detergents. Provide more comfort and natural look than you ever thought possible. Fleshtone.

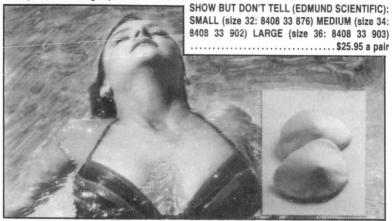

PHONIES. "Yehudi, a *busy signal* is more interesting than the message on *your* answering machine." Tired of listening to your friends complain about your messages? Let a celebrity answer your phone instead! Put on Richard Nixon (he's no crook), or Clark Gable (frankly, he doesn't give a damn). With these Rich Little impersonations, you can have any of two dozen famous people taking your calls. No more hang ups! Twelve 15-second messages are funny, tasteful. Transfer to any answering machine from your cassette player.

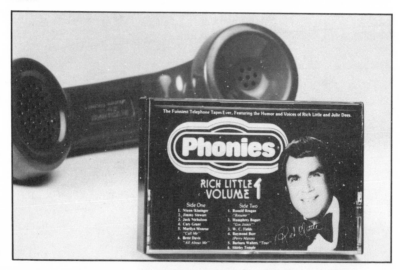

PERSONALIZED CHOCOLATE CHIP COOKIE. Here's a letter from a very satisfied customer that we'd like to share with you (intimate language has been deleted): "My girlfriend Charlene and I were really having trouble. She wouldn't !!$##! and that was nearly the end. That is, until I sent her one of your delicious 1-lb., heart-shaped, 12" chocolate chip cookies. I don't know if it was the personalized message or the absolutely delicious cookie that did the trick, but things sure have changed. Sometimes the only way to say it is with dough. Signed,———." Packed carefully to ensure freshness and guard against breakage. Made from all natural ingredients. Specify name.
COOKIE (ADAM YORK, Z981894D) $15.00

FRENCH SERVICE. . . . When "Oui" is enough. We enjoy playing maid and butler—we know you will too. Charming maid and butler G-strings, stretch nylon in black and white. Maid, one size fits 4 to 7; butler, one size.
MAID (NIGHT 'N' DAY INTIMATES, Z884304)...................... $12.00
BUTLER (Z884296)............. $12.00

ORDER BY PHONE

SPACE AGE SLIMMER BELT. Space may be the final frontier. But if you're so fat that your navel looks like it needs a toll booth in front of it, you'll never be a celestial pioneer. But never fear, space age slimmer belt is here! Holds in body heat to encourage fluid loss; washable Silvertex with soft, bonded lining; Velcro closure. 9″ w., adjustable, fits-all size. **SPACE AGE SLIMMER BELT (HANOVER HOUSE, Women's 24–36″ waist Z534189, Men's 36–48″ waist Z534206)** .... **$4.99; 2/$9.00**

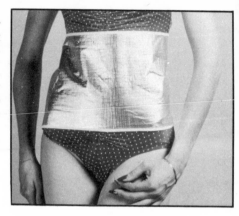

BUILD YOUR OWN PERISCOPE AND SET YOUR SIGHTS ABOVE THE CROWD! This sturdy periscope kit includes 2 mirrors, die-cut fiber board, and instructions for easy construction. Use for fun—or profit: Rent it at parades to short people. Up periscope! Down boredom! 14½″ × 2¾″ × 2¾″.
PERISCOPE (EDMUND SCIENTIFIC, ...
8408 31 788) **$9.95**
Pkg. of 10 (8408 31 955) **$84.95**

YOUR OWN PERSONAL PORTABLE SAUNA STEAM BATH. Pictured is Ivy Sedgwick, with her secretary, James, pampering herself in this luxurious sauna—without leaving the office! Folds compactly. Includes a UL-listed steam generator. Steel reinforced zippered top; automatic shut-off; plugs into any outlet. Extra durable vinyl. 39½″ × 23″. Convenient to enjoy in home or office! "James, take a letter. . . ."
SAUNA STEAM BATH. ....
(EDMUND SCIENTIFIC, 8408 31 963) $39.95

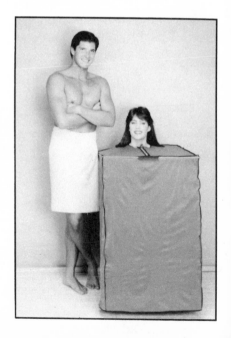

**GIANT PANORAMIC REARVIEW MIR-
ROR.** Stop depriving yourself! See vis-
tas you've never seen before! With
this Giant Panoramic Rearview Mirror
in your car gaze rearward and behold—The Great Behind! Enjoy the
adventure of this full and ripe visual
experience. Good for people with very
large eyebrows. Clips over present
mirror; flips to night for headlight
glare; ends unsightly blind spots.
**6-LANE MIRROR (HANOVER HOUSE,
Z484709)........................$4.88**

AT LAST—COMMUTER'S REVENGE!
Cut off on the freeway again?
These bright red and white gloves
send a message even the most
obnoxious driver can't miss. New
York City cab driver tested and ap-
proved. Made of acrylic blend, one
size fits all.
**FREEWAY GLOVES (KRUPP'S,
ACFU1) $7.50**

TRENCH COAT. "Pictured is my husband, Ralph, who one day went off to
work dressed in a leisure suit, and re-
turned wearing this beautifully detailed, elegantly fitted, fully lined,
water-resistant poly/cotton trench
coat. He *is* looking a bit doggy, although he never dressed so well
before." Features epaulet accents,
genuine leather buttons, large ample
collar. Tan; 16 only. *Personalized.*
TRENCH COAT (GEORGE'S 1010) $19.50

PEACH! — THE FINAL FRONTIER

These are the voyages of the Arctic Peach. Its mission: to seek out new climates, investigate new continents. To boldly grow where no peach has grown before. Developed by the University of New Hampshire, these peaches thrive in temperatures as low as 25 degrees below zero. Ripening in mid-August, the Arctic Peach has proved vigorous, honey sweet, fat growing, plump, and juicy.

ARCTIC PEACH (LAKELAND, Z171017E)..... Each $9.95; 2/$17.99; 3/$25.49; 4/$32.00

ANIMAL FACE GLASSES. Representative Jonathan C.B. Elliot (R) has proposed passage of the EZ Party Identification Bill mandating all Americans to don these Republican Elephant or Democratic Donkey Animal Face Glasses for instant public recognition. Says the congressman, "We Republicans love to play with our trunks."

**ELEPHANT GLASSES.................
(JOHNSON-SMITH, 4794M)....... $11.98
DONKEY GLASSES (4796M) $11.98**

ALL SYSTEMS ARE GO ABOARD THE SPACE SHUTTLE. Luckily you'll have read your *Space Shuttle Operator's Manual,* prepared with the assistance of the staff of NASA. Arranged to follow your flight every step of the way. Includes specific details on launch and ascent, Tang preparation, personal hygiene, working in space, pizza tossing in zero gravity, emergency procedures, entry and landing, and much more. With giant fold-outs of authentic orbital map and flight deck console. And at least you'll know when to check the oil. Giant 8½" × 11" paperback. 145 pages.
SPACE SHUTTLE MANUAL (JOHNSON-SMITH, 1797)...................................$11.95

WHAT WAS THE HEADLINE ON THE DAY *YOU* WERE BORN? Remember that classic "Headless Man in Topless Bar"? To find out what made the news on *your* birthday get one of these high-quality photographic silver prints (not Xerox copies). Includes any date from 1861 (for you centenarians—Civil War memories) to present. Specify year, month, and day. (Allow 4 weeks.)

BIRTHDAY NEWSPAPER (BOLIND)..............
11″ × 14″ Unframed (D3769A)............. $21.95
11″ × 14″ Framed (D3769B)............... $44.95
17″ × 23″ Unframed (D3769C)............. $29.95
17″ × 23″ Framed (D3769D)............... $59.95

SPACE GUN RADIO FLASHLIGHT. Set this laser gun to stun, and tune in with this space gun solid-state AM radio. Emits a bright beam of light—for reading or fun— when trigger is pulled. Requires ear plug, included. Operates on 2 "AA" batteries, not included. "Honey, I just want to relax tonight and listen to my gun."
GUN RADIO (JOHNSON-SMITH, 4784M)
.... $8.98

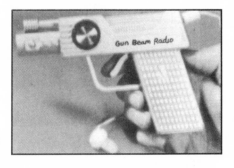

STAR TREK: THE ROLE PLAYING GAME. Voyage on the USS Enterprise! Assume the identity of *your* favorite character. Picture yourself as "Bones" saying, "He's dead, Jim." Or as the frantic Scottie: "Captain, I can't hold herrr togetherr much longerrr!" Or the heroic Captain James T. Kirk, "Beam me up, Scottie." Game after game of adventure and life-and-death situations—limited only by your imagination! 2 games available for 3 or more players, each containing game manual and everything you need.
BASIC STAR TREK GAME..................
(JOHNSON-SMITH, 7657M).......... $11.98
ADVANCED GAME (7658M).......... $24.98

EYESCOPE. If you're like us, seeing the inside of your own eye has been a lifelong dream. The eye is the window of the soul, and the Eyescope is the optical device to get you there. This specially designed diffuser incorporates a parabolic mirror and lens light. Beige. Note: Beauty is in the eye of the beholder.
EYESCOPE (EDMUND SCIENTIFIC, 8408 33 538) **$24.98**

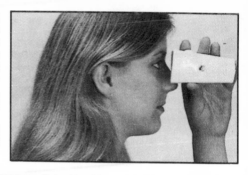

SAVON FEUILLE. Holy chic, thin soap from France—the new fashion trend in cleanliness! Each 2″ × 3″ packet contains 15 paper-thin sheets of soluble soap. Just whip it out and lather yourself into oblivion. With cover illustration by Peter Paul Rubens, suitable for framing (parental guidance suggested). Great for you Francophiles, and it sure beats heisting those mini-bars from French hotels. Instructions in English, Dutch, and, of course, French (sank goodness).
3 PACKETS OF SOAP (JERRYCO, J-2659-3) $2.25 (0.1 lbs.)
(24 J-2659-24) .... **$14.40 (0.7 lbs.)**

FAKE BULLET HOLES. With these realistic decals stuck to the windshield of your Corvette, you'll really impress your girlfriend. "Oh, Butch, it looks like you've been shot at! You're a real pistol!" "Yeah, baby, so squeeze a little closer before it's too late." 15 per package.
BULLET HOLES (JOHNSON-SMITH, 2246) **$0.98**

WOODEN DUMMY ROUND. Just in time for the new decorating season, we bring you this glorious oak and maple wooden dummy round. Some people are naturally chic. *You* can be too with these super rounds in your home. Each dummy is 35″ long and just under 25 lbs. Use as an "I mean business" doorstop; great for artillery aerobics, too. Or stave off trespassers—just yell, "I've got the ammunition, honey—you get the gun!"
WOODEN DUMMY ROUND (JERRYCO, J-5012-1) .... **$45.00, postage and handling included.**

FINALLY SOMETHING FOR YOU FLATHEADS! Is your head so flat it's mistaken for an end table? Your dome so horizontal that you're nicknamed "Skillets"? Never have a lonely Saturday night again with this 14" pointed flesh-colored conehead disguise. Made of the finest quality rubber, it's guaranteed to retain its shape. "Wig" completely covers front of head and about halfway down back of neck; hides sideburns as well. Pointy heads are sexy.
CONEHEAD DISGUISE (JOHNSON-SMITH, 4705) $6.98

AT LAST! IT'S EYE PHONES—the sensory deprivation experience! Just kick off your shoes, and put on this over-size eyemask. Plug the ear cord into a sound source, sit back, and relax to your favorite music. Or get Eye Phones for each member of the family—and experience nothingness as a family unit! So refreshing. Afterward, have a family discussion(?). Comes with Walkman-type cord and stereo mini-plug, with an adapter for full-size stereo jacks.
EYE PHONES (UNIQUITY, AM249-00) $16.95

SOUND LIKE AN AMBULANCE. Or a squad car, or a fire truck—with this new well-made, battery-operated bike siren and loudspeaker. You'll get such satisfaction when you scream through your bullhorn, "Get out of the way, you turkey! You drive like you're from Jersey!" Hope you have a good attorney. 4" unit bracket fits any bike.
SIREN AND LOUDSPEAKER (JOAN COOK, B1554) $9.00

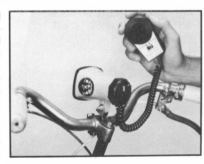

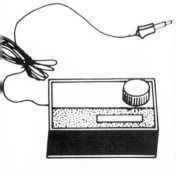

NO JIVE BROADCAST SCAM SET. Yo, Jim, you wanna be a D.J.? Tune into this rap, Jack: Just plug this AM transmitter into the earphone jack of your cassette player. You can broadcast your tape onto any AM radio by simply turning the knob to the AM station you choose. The jack acts as a switch, the cord as an antenna; your range is only 10', so you'll have a select audience. But won't they be rockin' and hip hip hoppin' with the vibes you'll send into their lives . . . hit it! (9-volt battery not incl.)
AM TRANSMITTER (JERRYCO, J-2381-1) . . . . $4.75 (0.2 lbs.)

THE TWO-POTATO CLOCK. Remember the oil embargo? Those gasoline lines? Maybe the answer to the global energy shortage is right in our own refrigerators: Spud Power. The Two-Potato Clock is on the cutting edge of the new Tater Technology. The Liquid Crystal Display Digital actually runs on the power of two potatoes; by inserting two electrodes, a voltage flow from the potatoes' acidic content forms current to power the clock. But this clock is just the beginning. There's news that the Russians may be developing a Spudnik already. Ireland could become a major tuber exporter, changing the balance of world power. Don't be the last on your block to enter the potato age. Note: clock also runs on apples, avocadoes, cucumbers, cola—even beer. Approx. 8½″ L × 3½″ W, with instructions.

TWO-POTATO CLOCK, (ADAM YORK, Z987420) **$15.00**

DOWN-FILLED ATHLETIC SUPPORTER. Keep your loved ones warm with this down-filled jock strap. No sense freezing anything important. After all, love means never having to say "It's frozen." Great for joggers, skiers, someone special. Top quality down. Washable. Attractively packaged. One size fits all.

DOWN SUPPORTER. ....
(JOHNSON-SMITH, 4777M) ... **$12.98**

BUY A FAMOUS PASSENGER! Mingle with the stars, with these lifesize cardboard photo look-alikes! With Marilyn in your car, you'll get looks, with Rodney Dangerfield, you'll get no respect, and Joan Rivers will keep you laughing! Spring-action hand waves whenever car's in motion. Self-adheres and removes instantly.

STARPOOL WAVERS (KRUPP'S,
.... **Marilyn Monroe TOC8)**
..... **(Rodney Dangerfield TOC9)**
(Joan Rivers TOC10) Each $8.00

BEAUTY BUST CREAM. Like a fine parquet floor, breasts too need to be oiled. With this special cream developed in Europe, help *your* bust retain a youthful appearance. Easy to use . . . simply slather on bust area daily.
BUST CREAM (HANOVER HOUSE, Z570739).........................$4.99

ENORMOUS WEATHER BALLOONS! "Hey, Mommy, look what I found! Can I keep it?" "Why, it's a 16-foot weather balloon . . . sure, dear, but you'll have to clean up after it."
BALLOONS (EDMUND SCIENTIFIC, Pkg of 2: 3-ft. size 8408 41 755)...$9.95
(8-ft. size 8408 60 568)............$9.95
(16-ft. size 8408 72 151).........$40.95

DOG WATERBED. Binky and Hanover Markson, two terrier cousins, broke the known world's record for bedrest by remaining prone on this marvelously comfortable canine water mattress (that fits inside a foam base) for an entire year. They have not been off the waterbed since its purchase date and they say, "We don't plan on budging yet. We've never enjoyed ourselves more, although there have been a few dog days, let me tell you." Washable outside cover is beige sheepskin-like fabric. Therapeutic value.
WATERBED (GEORGE'S, 3016)
26″ × 16″ $45.00
40″ × 26″ $66.00

POCKET MICROSCOPE. "Geez, Freddie, ever wonder how many grains of salt there are on a potato chip? I can tell you with my pocket microscope—makes close inspection a snap!" 25X microscope is only 5″ long with brushed aluminum finish and pocket clip. Precision ground lens system gives distortion-free detail and powerful magnification, and clear plastic mount makes for a quick clear view. "Nine thousand fifty-six, nine thousand fifty-seven . . ."
POCKET MICROSCOPE.....................
(EDMUND SCIENTIFIC, 8404 31 853) $10.95; 3/$15.95; 6/$29.95

THE PIG HAT™. Pictured are Mr. and Mrs. Norman Oinkleworth. When he proposed marriage, the condition of her acceptance was that they continue her family tradition: to always wear these wonderful Pig Hats™ in public, and to feed on corn husk chowder from a trough on Fridays. Not being pigheaded, he happily agreed. Now you can wear one too. Adjustable. One size fits all.
PIG HAT™ **(HOG WILD!) $9.95**

$AMAZING PRICES!$

SAILOR COAT. "Prudence, gosh honey, dress the dog for our yacht trip today. Go get his navy blue with white trim water-repellent sailor coat—you know, the one that's fully lined. With all of his drooling, panting, sniffing, and scratching, at least he'll be properly dressed." *Personalized.*
SAILOR COAT (GEORGE'S, 1002)
Sizes 10 through 16 ....$17.50

64

SLINGSHOT AGE USHERED IN! Ret. Col. Beryl Peabody was the first man to sling himself across the English Channel in a slingshot made from this 82"-circumference giant rubber band. Said Peabody, "What an exhilarating feeling! Like flying, rather. A tricky business, what?" All we can say is, one small step for man, one giant snap for mankind. Rubber band comes in military foil sack.
GIANT RUBBER BAND (JERRYCO, J-2327-1)
.... $2.50 (0.5 lbs.)

WOLF WHISTLE. "Gosh, Marv, wish we could get that pretty girl's attention." "Stan, since the beginning of time, man has used animal calls to catch his prey. Like the wild moose or duck, women respond to calls, too. With this wolf whistle I can lure just the girls I want. Perfect for cruising the streets, it fits in the palm of my hand, or in my pocket. Just use the whistle and watch! Wee-woo! WOW, another great catch."
WOLF WHISTLE (JOHNSON-SMITH, 2116) $1.98

PIG EARRINGS AND TACK/PIN. In a sow's ear, you say? No, in *your* ear! Display your porker preference proudly on your ear lobes and chest by wearing these pig earrings and pin. Pigs are great and the whole world should know it! So show it! Pink, of course.
SOW'S EARS (HOG WILD!).............. $6.95
TACK/PIN............................. $3.95

COSMETIC VEIL. "Oh, darn! While doing my Jane Fonda exercises I got lipstick on my socks again!" Hold everything! Does this scenario sound all too familiar? Try Cosmetic Veil and avoid smudging makeup. Slips over head and ties. Nylon tricot. Can also be used as individual mosquito netting, beehive keeper's mask, or food sieve.
COSMETIC VEIL (BOLIND, D4219) .... $7.95; 2/$15.50

65

GIANT FLY. Modeled after the treacherous Brazilian Cupcake Feeder Fly, this 7"-long replica is ugly, frightening, and oh-so realistic. Complete with hairy legs, transparent wings, and a suction cup so you can stick it anywhere.
GIANT FLY (JOHNSON-SMITH, 2035N) $3.50

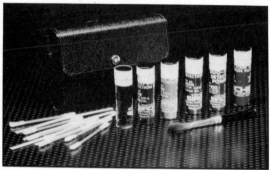

AT LONG LAST! Here's a complete kit with all the necessary dyes for creating an entrapment situation. For revenge, fun, or profit! These dyes are tough, too! They defy even the most powerful detergents and cleaning. Comes with a carrying case for those on-the-go entrapments. With instructions on how to use the supplies to catch *your* next victim. Great fun for the whole family!
SNARE KIT (EDMUND SCIENTIFIC, 8408 33 584) $49.00

HEIGHT BUILDERS. "Honey, you look . . . different. Have you grown taller? I never looked into your navel before." Only you know the secret: Elevator Height Increase Pads. Slip into any shoe. They're scientifically designed, comfortable, lightweight, and best of all, invisible.
HEIGHT BUILDERS (JOHNSON-SMITH, 4027M) $4.98

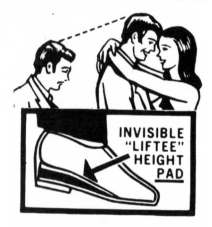

INVISIBLE "LIFTEE" HEIGHT PAD

MUSICAL ROSE. Nothing says it better than flowers. But sentiments can wane as flowers wilt and die. But wait! At last the perfect musical bloom that lasts as long as true love itself. Gosh. Twist it on to fill the air with music for lovers as it glows a deep red. 11½" high. Batteries not included. Assorted tunes. Beautiful music, sweet romance.
MUSICAL ROSE (RAINBOW OF GIFTS, Z710004). . . . .
. . . . $5.99 each; set of 2/$10.99

AUTOMATIC FLY ZAPPER. Going fly hunting with the kids again, Renfield? Take along this spring-activated fly shooter with line. You can use it again and again. Made of 3½″-long hard-hitting mesh, this missile zapper really kills flies dead. They're fun to hunt, and make great eating, too.
FLY ZAPPER (JOHNSON-SMITH, 6294M)
.... **$3.98**

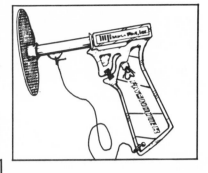

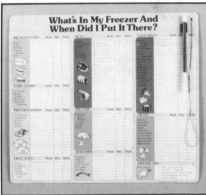

FREEZER CHECKLIST. "Oh, Cora, is that pork butt still in the freezer?" Men can be so annoying! Eliminate those nagging meal-time questions. "Check my freezer checklist and see for yourself," you'll be able to say.... Now you'll know your freezer's contents at a glance, where food is, date stored, description ... even freezer tips. Magnetized board, slick wipe-clean surface. Marker pencil attached. 16″ × 14″.
FREEZER CHECKLIST (COLONIAL GARDEN KITCHENS, 3-4100) **$6.95**

DOG FORTUNE COOKIES. What better way to top off your dog's shrimp in lobster sauce dinner with cold noodles in sesame paste, than with authentic doggie fortune cookies? A real surprise treat! Hmmm, what will his fortune be? You'll probably have to read it to him ...
FORTUNE COOKIES (GEORGE'S, 6034) **$1.90**

ONION MAGIC GOGGLES & BOOK. Since Biblical times, humankind has wept, wailed, cried, and sobbed when handling onions. What a sorry sight!—for it is written that thou shalt weepeth when peelingeth thy onions. But weepeth no more—with onion goggles! Protect thine eyes and cooketh delicious meals with *Onion Magic,* a 64-page recipe book including everything from onion appetizers to main dishes.
GOGGLES & BOOK (BOLIND, 4204) **$11.50**

ELEPHANT GARLIC!

Holy pachyderm! Hold your nose! Each clove matures into mammoth full-size bud by the second year; sections divide like tangerines. Sold in sets of 3, this variety keeps indefinitely, grows anywhere, and is sub-zero hardy. You'll appreciate the subtle, mild-yet-tangy flavor. Great for main dishes, or as a side dish. "Oh, honey, I'll have a second helping—of garlic." Caution: your breath may be hazardous to friends' health.

ELEPHANT GARLIC (LAKELAND, Z000182Y)................$2.49; 2/$4.49; 4/$8.49

BUDWEISER CAMERA. After a long, hard day's work, sit back and enjoy a brew. But wait! This isn't a real brew—it's a camera! This no-deposit, no-return Bud camera can easily be disguised in a 6-pack of brew. Great for uncanny shots. Whatever you do, *this* Bud's for you. 110 print or slide film, easy to operate, handy carrying strap.

BUDWEISER CAMERA (OLD VILLAGE, Z566026)...........................$19.99

STAR WORLDS. Want to kiss under the stars? Why not turn on this home planetarium and light the ceiling of your room. Put the universe where it belongs—indoors! With it's rotating globe, star charts, lighted pointer, and astronomy booklet it will be so romantic—and enlightening! 8½″ × 8½″ × 16½″. Uses flashlight bulb and 2 "D" batteries.

STAR WORLDS (EDMUND SCIENTIFIC,........ 8408 31 891)...........................$39.95

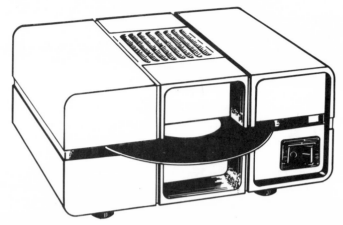

IT'S ODORIFIC! Sniff your way out of that ratty old rec room reeking of stale beer, smelly socks, dirty laundry, old TV dinners. With these fabulous fragrances relive that lusty weekend by the sea or that blustery romantic evening in front of the fireplace when a fire was burning in more than the hearth. With the Aroma Discs and Disc Player you can turn on your favorite smell for an hour of odor pleasure. Two sample discs come with the player. Aroma discs are the next best thing to being there—maybe even better. Replacement Aroma Disc pack contains 5 different short-play fragrance records: mountain-top, seaside, open field, fireplace, roses.

AROMA DISC PLAYER (KRUPP'S, HOROMA). **$29.95**
REPLACEMENT DISCS (INRE6) **$14.00**

PHONY LADIES LEGS. "Gunter, did you know that there's a pair of phony ladies legs sticking out of your shorts?" "Yes, I carry them in my pocket so that I can put them in embarrassing places—like under a bed or in a closet. I can use them over and over again. They're made of inflatable vinyl and are about 36" long. I bet you could use a pair for your shorts, too! But sorry, only 1 pair per set."
PHONY LEGS (JOHNSON-SMITH, 3018) **$6.98**

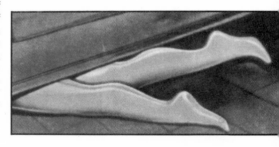

THE EAR YOU SAVE MAY BE YOUR OWN. "Honey, did you feed the dog today?" "No, dear, I didn't have too. He ate his ear." Stop! This can't be true! And it isn't. These bowls are made especially to prevent the above scene from ever happening. Made of heavyweight durable plastic with rubber feet to prevent skidding; dishwasher safe, indoor or outdoor use. Almond, Yellow, or Brown. *Personalized.* 7¾".
LONG EARED PERSONALIZED BOWL (GEORGE'S, 4013). **$6.20**

SEE STARS WITHOUT RECEIVING BLOW TO HEAD! "Look, Johnny Mae, it's the Milky Way!" Wrong, Janie Sue, you could use a pair of glasses. It's 150 glow-in-the-dark decals of stars, planets, and comets you can attach to *your* bedroom ceiling in a jiffy. Educational, too, Janie Sue, 'cause it includes a chart of the heavens.
TWINKLING STAR CEILING ....
(HANOVER HOUSE, Z361550).........$1.49

STOP SNORING NOW! News Flash: Thunderous snores register 8.6 on the Richter scale, causing massive landslides in the Santa Denida Valley. Sound like you? If so, try this doctor-tested collar. Made of soft foam, it keeps chin from dropping and partially blocks windpipe, preventing the cause of snoring. Velcro close, washable cover. It could save your marriage.
STOP SNORING NOW (MATURE WISDOM, Z359734)............................$7.99

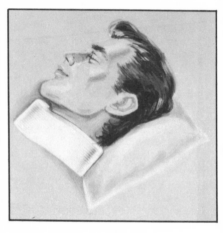

 *THIS COULD BE YOURS!*

THE BIG DRIP RAIN LAMP. Luciano Veneto of Brooklyn, N.Y., on The Big Drip Rain Lamp: "It's so wet! I said to myself, 'Self-a, how do they do it? That golden Venus, she's-a always bathed by-a drippety drop drop?'" Well, Luciano, the secret lies in a special oil that "rains" continuously, and a pump that is concealed in the lamp. Bronze finish steel with golden chain. On/off switch. 6½" dia., 16" h.
SWAG LAMP (HANOVER HOUSE, Z707331)
....................................$29.99

FOAM RUBBER WIND CHIMES, "Silent Vigil"™. When you love the looks but hate the sound! These lovely blue foam rubber wind chimes make a great display piece for the contemporary home. Eliminate the bothersome clanging of ordinary wind chimes. People may laugh at you, but they've laughed at you before. Approx 10″ H.
FOAM RUBBER WIND CHIMES (BOLIND, 4175)
.... $5.95; 2/$11.50

THE THINKING LIGHT SWITCH. "I've been in the Breaking & Entering business for the past 35 years, but this is the first time I've been foiled by a smart light!"—Frankie the Slim Jim, San Quentin. An excellent device for scaring away intruders. The Audiolite is the same size as a regular light switch and goes on with the slightest sound. Stays on if noise continues. An adjustable timer keeps light on for 7 seconds to 7 minutes. UL approved.
AUDIOLITE (EDMUND SCIENTIFIC) for incandescent lighting up to 300 watts (8408 31 912)
.... **$34.95**
AUDIOLITE for fluorescent lighting (8408 33 023)
.... **$34.95**
4 units of either........................ **$99.00**

CLASSICAL COMPOSER CARDS. Ever wonder if Bach played strip poker? Maybe not, but now *you* can play strip poker with him—and Beethoven and Mozart. Wow, that's hot! This standard playing deck features 54 composers' portraits, and their birth and death dates; music motif on back. Never again experience the utter humiliation of not knowing Beethoven's birthday. We know this deck doesn't include all of your favorites (and ours), like Marvin Hamlisch, Henry Mancini, and Barry Manilow. But what do you want for $3.99? A class(ical) act!
CLASSICAL COMPOSER CARDS..............
(HANOVER HOUSE, Z558395) **$3.99**

ACUPUNCTURE DOLL. Discovered at Schlomo Goldstein's Acupuncture & Body Work Shop, this acupuncture doll makes a great companion for the hypochondriac. The 10¾"-high, wire-reinforced doll is numbered all over its body and comes with an extensive (if difficult to read) guide to hundreds of puncture points for all sorts of ailments. There is no acupuncture cure, however, for poverty or bad judgment.
ACUPUNCTURE DOLL (JERRYCO, J-1892-1) .... $4.25 (0.7 lbs.)

WE JUST GET BETTER AND BETTER. The Pith Helmet Car John is the newest and most technologically advanced Car John in the world. Evolved from the original and widely acclaimed Car John (see page 7), this one's for the whole family (not all at once)! Easy storage—just detach army helmet and wear as fashion accessory. Sturdy 16-oz. styrene reservoir with tube.
PITH HELMET CAR JOHN (HANOVER HOUSE, Z492652) $4.99

WOMEN'S FACIAL ELECTROLYSIS WAND. No more ugly long hairs! Get tough with those pesky quill-like hairs on chin and elsewhere. This electrolysis wand promises smooth skin with the touch of its electric prong. Never again exclaim in dismay, "Gosh, that hair is ugly." Now you'll say, "Quick, hand me my Wand!" Batteries included.
HAIR REMOVER (OLD VILLAGE, Z338939) $9.99

SOLAR POWERED AIR-CONDITIONED SAFARI HAT. Employing the energy of our most powerful natural resource, the sun, this hat eliminates the need for central air conditioning. This beautifully made, desert-sand color, traditional British explorer's helmet runs in daylight on six ½-volt solar cells with unlimited life, and at night or indoors on auxiliary battery power (2 "AA" cells not incl.). The motor-driven fan operates an evaporating continuously circulating cooling system. Stops perspiration, keeps away insects, dust, fumes. Adjustable headband, one size fits all. Lightweight 8 oz. Keep cool and righteous knowing that tomorrow's energy solution is resting on your head. Coming soon: solar powered air-conditioned training bra.
SAFARI HAT (JOHNSON-SMITH, 6584M)..... $89.98

THE THINKING MECHANICAL PENCIL CALCULATOR. With this smart pencil you can automatically get exact answers to addition, subtraction, multiplication, division, and square root problems. And believe it or not, this pencil can also write and draw lines. When placed behind ear it'll make you look as smart as it is. Even if you're not. Attractive aluminum finish. 6½" long.
PENCIL CALCULATOR (JOHNSON-SMITH, 4024) $3.98

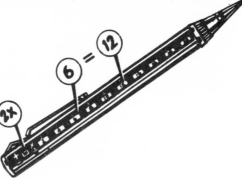

DOESN'T EVERYONE DESERVE A LULLABY? Even your plants, those sensitive little creatures that can be so easily over- or under-watered. Never under-water again with Plant Sentry. It plays a soft, gentle melody to tell you it's the right time to water. 11" long and needle shaped so you can place it in soil next to plant without damage to root structure. Fill the whole nursery with them! Battery operated (with 1.5V "AA" battery, not incl.).
PLANT SENTRY (EDMUND SCIENTIFIC, ... 8408 33 772) ..... $14.95; 2/$12.95 each; 4 or more/$9.95 each.

POCKET PEN RADIO. Next time your pal asks, "Did you hear that new hit song by Wayne Newton?" you can say "Yes—on my handy pen. It's a real working radio with a tiny earphone for listening. Guaranteed to pull in stations in our area, although reception varies from place to place. I don't need batteries, so there's no additional expense. It's a selfpowered solid state circuit with a germanium diode and it comes with ground wire (though it isn't always necessary). Best of all, it comes complete and ready to play." "Gosh, I just asked a simple question. . . ."
PEN RADIO (JOHNSON-SMITH, 7052).....$5.98

LIFE A LITTLE NOISY FOR YOU? Mask out the maddening roar of daily life with Sound Conditioner—creates a contemplative environment with restful background sounds. Four controls and channels. *Surf 1:* repeating pattern. *Surf 2:* random wave pattern. *Rain:* downpour. *Waterfall.* 5½" × 7½" × 6½". Surf's up! Sanity's back! Great for light sleepers, city dwellers, psychiatrists.
SOUND CONDITIONER (EDMUND SCIENTIFIC, 8408 72 293)........$129.00

SNOUT GLASSES™. These new, deluxe disguise glasses for traveling "inhognito" can now be yours. No one will recognize you! Great for illicit rendezvous or for avoiding bill collectors. Who's the man in the pig glasses? they'll ask. Only you will know. . . . One size fits all. Two pair.
SNOUT GLASSES™ (HOG WILD!).....$5.95

HOW TO ORDER FROM THIS BOOK

Select the item you would like to order. In the catalog copy, the last line indicates the Item name, the Company name and Ordering Number set in parentheses, and the Price. For example, if you would like to order the Sunbrella Hat, the company is Old Village, the ordering number is A460204, and the price is $3.88. The companies and their ordering information are listed here alphabetically. So you would turn to the page with the Old Village listing.

Using our order form, fill in your name, the company name, and the ordering information. Remember that you *cannot* order from two different companies on one order form. Each company requires a separate order form. Please be sure you place your order to the correct company. You can make copies of our order form for additional ordering, or you can call in orders.

Neither we nor the mail order companies can be held responsible for misplaced orders, so order carefully. DO NOT SEND CASH!

The following companies are represented in this catalog, and ordering information can be found alphabetically: **ADAM YORK, BRUCE BOLIND, COLONIAL GARDEN KITCHENS, EDMUND SCIENTIFIC, THE FULL DECK, GEORGE'S, HANOVER HOUSE, HOG WILD!, JERRYCO, JOAN COOK, JOHNSON-SMITH, KRUPP'S, LAKELAND NURSERIES, MATURE WISDOM, NIGHT 'N' DAY INTIMATES, OLD VILLAGE SHOP, PENNSYLVANIA STATION, RAINBOW OF GIFTS, TAPESTRY, UNIQUITY.**

ADAM YORK, Unique Merchandise Mart, Building 6, Hanover, PA 17333 (717) 637-1600 (C.C. orders: 1-800-621-5800)

Postage/Handling:	Merchandise	Add
	up to $20.00	$2.95
	$20.01–$30.00	$3.95
	$30.01–$40.00	$4.95
	$40.01–$50.00	$5.95
	$50.01–$75.00	$7.50
	over $75.00	$8.25

Add 95¢ Insurance on all orders. Pennsylvania residents add 6% sales tax. Items lost or damaged in transit will be replaced free. On orders of $15.00 up C.C. accepted: AMEX, CARTE BLANCHE, DINERS CLUB, MASTERCARD, VISA.

BRUCE BOLIND, 185 Bolind Building, P.O. Box 9751, Boulder, CO 80301 (303) 443-9688

Postage/Handling:	Merchandise	Add
	up to $4.99	$0.95
	$5.00–$9.99	$1.95
	$10.00–$19.99	$2.95
	$20.00–$29.99	$3.80
	$30.00–$39.99	$4.35
	$40.00–$49.99	$4.75
	$50.00–$99.99	$5.45
	$100.00 and over	$6.45

Colorado residents add 3.6% sales tax. On orders of $10.00 up C.C. accepted: MASTERCARD, VISA.

COLONIAL GARDEN KITCHENS, Dept. M5DRS, 270 West Merrick Road, Valley Stream, NY 11582 Toll Free Number 1-800-645-2978

Postage/Handling:	Merchandise	Add
	up to $10.00	$2.45
	$10.01–$15.00	$2.80
	$15.01–$20.00	$3.30
	$20.01–$30.00	$4.30
	$30.01–$35.00	$4.55
	$35.01–$45.00	$4.80
	$45.01–$99.00	$5.80
	over $100.00	$6.80

New York State residents add sales tax. On orders of $15.00 up C.C. accepted: AMEX, MASTERCARD, VISA.

EDMUND SCIENTIFIC CO., 101 E. Gloucester Pike, Barrington, NJ 08007 (609) 547-3488

Postage/Handling:

Merchandise	Add
up to $19.99	$2.95
$20.00–$29.99	$3.95
$30.00–$39.99	$4.95
$40.00–$49.99	$5.95
$50.00–$99.99	$6.95
$100.00–$199.99	$7.95
$200.00 and over	$9.95

Add 85¢ Insurance to all orders. New Jersey residents add 6% sales tax. Items lost or damaged in transit will be replaced free. C.C. accepted: AMEX, CARTE BLANCHE, DINERS CLUB, MASTERCARD, VISA.

THE FULL DECK, 80 Charles Street, New York, NY 10014 (212) 989-7434
Price: $3.50 per deck, shipping included. Allow 2 weeks for delivery. For "A Pack of Lies!" only.

GEORGE'S, 2407 Wolfangle Road, Cincinnati, OH 45244 (606) 635-3376

Postage/Handling:

Merchandise	Add
up to $10.00	$2.00
$10.01–$50.00	$4.00
over $50.00	no charge

Ohio residents add 5½% sales tax. On orders of $20.00 up C.C. accepted: MASTERCARD, VISA.

HANOVER HOUSE, Unique Merchandise Mart, Building 2, Hanover, PA 17333 (717) 637-1600

Postage/Handling:

Merchandise	Add
up to $10.00	$2.49
$10.01–$20.00	$3.69
$20.01–$30.00	$4.49
over $30.00	$4.99

Add 95¢ Insurance to all orders. Pennsylvania residents add 6% sales tax. Items lost or damaged in transit will be replaced free. On orders of $10.00 up C.C. accepted: AMEX, CARTE BLANCHE, DINERS CLUB, MASTERCARD, VISA.

HOG WILD!, 280 Friend Street, Boston, MA 02114 (617) 523-7447

Postage/Handling:

Merchandise	Add
up to $27.50	$2.50
$27.51–$55.00	$4.25
$55.01–$110.00	$5.75
$110.01–$225.00	$6.95
over $225.00	3½% of total

Massachusetts residents add 5% sales tax. C.C. accepted: AMEX, MASTERCARD, VISA.

JERRYCO, INC., 601 Linden Place, Evanston, IL 60202 (312) 475-8440

Postage/Handling:

Merchandise	Add
1 lb.–5 lbs.	$2.18
6 lbs.–10 lbs.	$3.15
11 lbs.–15 lbs.	$4.13
16 lbs.–20 lbs.	$5.10
21 lbs.–25 lbs.	$6.08
26 lbs.–30 lbs.	$7.05
31 lbs.–35 lbs.	$8.03
36 lbs.–40 lbs.	$9.00
41 lbs.–45 lbs.	$9.98
46 lbs.–50 lbs.	$10.95

Illinois residents add 7% sales tax. $10.00 minimum on all orders, including shipping. C.C. accepted: MASTERCARD, VISA.

JOAN COOK, P.O. Box 21628, Ft. Lauderdale, FL 33335-1628 1-800-327-3799 (Ft. Lauderdale: 766-8400)

Postage/Handling:

Merchandise	Add
up to $20.00	$3.95
$21.00–$30.00	$4.45
$31.00–$50.00	$5.45
$51.00–$75.00	$5.95
$76.00–$99.00	$6.45
over $100.00 no charge, we pay postage	

Florida residents add 5% sales tax. Add $2.00 per item for gift wrapping. On orders of $20.00 up C.C. accepted: AMEX, MASTERCARD, VISA.

JOHNSON-SMITH, 35075 Automation Drive, Mt. Clemens, MI 48043 C.C. orders: (313) 791-2805

Postage/Handling:

Merchandise	Add
up to $3.00	$0.75
$3.01–$6.00	$1.70
$6.01–$10.00	$2.25
$10.01–$15.00	$2.65
$15.01–$20.00	$3.40
$20.01–$30.00	$3.75
over $30.00	$3.95

Michigan residents add 4% sales tax. On orders of $10.00 up C.C. accepted: MASTERCARD, VISA.

KRUPP'S MAIL ORDER, P.O. Box 9090, Boulder, CO 80301 (303) 443-8700

Postage/Handling:

Merchandise	Add: Fast	Superfast
$5.00–$9.99	$2.35	$5.25
$10.00–$14.99	$3.00	$5.75
$15.00–$24.99	$3.75	$6.75
$25.00–49.99	$4.25	$7.50
$50.00–74.99	$5.25	$8.50
over $75.00	$6.75	$10.00

Colorado residents add 6.15% sales tax. No orders under $5.00. C.C. accepted: MASTERCARD, VISA.

LAKELAND NURSERIES, Unique Merchandise Mart, Building 4, Hanover, PA 17333 (717) 637-1600

Postage/Handling:

Merchandise	Add
up to $5.00	$1.95
$5.01–$10.00	$2.95
$10.01–$15.00	$3.95
$15.01–$20.00	$4.95
$20.01–$30.00	$5.75
over $30.01	$6.75

Add 95¢ Insurance to all orders. Pennsylvania residents add 6% sales tax. Items lost or damaged in transit will be replaced free. On orders of $10.00 up C.C. accepted: AMEX, CARTE BLANCHE, DINERS CLUB, MASTERCARD, VISA.

MATURE WISDOM, Unique Merchandise Mart, Building 28, Hanover, PA 17333 (717) 637-1600 (C.C. orders: 1-800-621-5800; IL: 1-800-972-5858)

Postage/Handling:

Merchandise	Add
up to $15.00	$2.99
$15.01–$25.00	$3.99
$25.01–$40.00	$4.99
over $40.00	$5.49

Add 95¢ Insurance to all orders. Pennsylvania residents add 6% sales tax. Items lost or damaged in transit will be replaced free. On orders of $10.00 up C.C. accepted: AMEX, CARTE BLANCHE, DINERS CLUB, MASTERCARD, VISA.

NIGHT 'N' DAY INTIMATES, Unique Merchandise Mart, Building 22, Hanover, PA 17333
1-800-621-5800 (IL: 1-800-972-5858)

Postage/Handling:

Merchandise	Add
up to $10.00	$1.75
$10.01–$25.00	$2.75
$25.01–$40.00	$3.75
$40.01–$60.00	$4.75
over $60.00	$6.00

Add 95¢ Insurance to all orders. No sales tax. Items lost or damaged in transit will be replaced free. On orders of $15.00 up C.C. accepted: AMEX, CARTE BLANCHE, DINERS CLUB, MASTERCARD, VISA.

OLD VILLAGE SHOP, Unique Merchandise Mart, Building 8, Hanover, PA 17333 (717) 637-1600 (C.C. orders: 1-800-621-5800; IL: 1-800-972-5858)

Postage/Handling:

Merchandise	Add
up to $15.00	$2.99
$15.01–$25.00	$3.99
$25.01–$40.00	$4.99
over $40.00	$5.49

Add 95¢ Insurance to all orders. Pennsylvania residents add 6% sales tax (excluding clothing). Items lost or damaged in transit will be replaced free. On orders of $10.00 up C.C. accepted: AMEX, CARTE BLANCHE, DINERS CLUB, MASTERCARD, VISA.

PENNSYLVANIA STATION, Unique Merchandise Mart, Building 14, Hanover, PA 17333 (717) 637-1600 (C.C. orders: 1-800-621-5800; IL: 1-800-972-5858)

Postage/Handling:

Merchandise	Add
up to $9.99	$1.95
$10.00–$19.99	$2.95
$20.00–$29.99	$3.95
$30.00–$39.99	$4.95
$40.00–$49.99	$5.95
$50.00–$75.00	$6.75
over $75.00	$7.75

Add 95¢ Insurance to all orders. Pennsylvania residents add 6% sales tax. Items lost or damaged in transit will be replaced free. On orders of $25.00 up C.C. accepted: AMEX, CARTE BLANCHE, DINERS CLUB, MASTERCARD, VISA.

RAINBOW OF GIFTS, Unique Merchandise Mart, Building 30, Hanover, PA 17333 (717) 637-1600 (C.C. orders: 1-800-821-5800; IL: 1-800-972-5858)

Postage/Handling:

Merchandise	Add
up to $15.00	$2.99
$15.01–$25.00	$3.99
$25.01–$40.00	$4.99
over $40.00	$5.49

Add 95¢ Insurance to all orders. Pennsylvania residents add 6% sales tax. Items lost or damaged in transit will be replaced free. On orders of $10.00 up C.C. accepted: AMEX, CARTE BLANCHE, DINERS CLUB, MASTERCARD, VISA.

TAPESTRY, Unique Merchandise Mart, Building 46, Hanover, PA 17333 (717) 637-1600 (C.C. orders: 1-800-621-5800; IL: 1-800-972-5858)

Postage/Handling:

Merchandise	Add
up to $20.00	$2.95
$20.01–$30.00	$3.95
$30.01–$40.00	$4.95
$40.01–$50.00	$5.95
$50.01–$75.00	$7.50
$75.01 and over	$8.25

Add 95¢ Insurance to all orders. Pennsylvania residents add 6% sales tax. Items lost or damaged in transit will be replaced free.

UNIQUITY, 215 4th Street, P.O. Box 6, Galt, CA 95632 (209) 745-2111

Postage/Handling:

Merchandise	Add/USA	Add/Canada & Mexico
$5.00–$15.00	$3.00	$7.50
$15.01–$25.00	$3.50	$9.00
$25.01–$50.00	$4.00	$10.50
$50.01–$100.00	$6.00	$14.00
$100.01–$200.00	$8.00	$15.00
$200.01 up	$10.00	$20.00

California residents add 6% sales tax. No orders under $5.00. On orders of $10.00 up C.C. accepted: MASTERCARD, VISA.

ORDER FORM ORDER FORM ORDER FORM ORDER FORM

THE ROTATING SPAGHETTI FORK
AND OTHER ITEMS YOU CAN'T LIVE WITHOUT

SEND MERCHANDISE TO:

NAME ______________________________

ADDRESS ______________________________

CITY/STATE ______________________ ZIP __________

DAYTIME TELEPHONE (   ) ______________________

ITEM ORDERED FROM: ______________________

COMPANY NAME/ADDRESS ______________________

____

ITEM NUMBER	HOW MANY	ITEM NAME/ DESCRIPTION	SIZE/ COLOR	PRICE

AMERICAN EXPRESS __________ VISA __________

MASTERCARD __________ BANK NO. __________

DINERS CLUB __________ CARTE BLANCHE __________

CREDIT CARD ACCT. NO.: __________

EXPIRATION DATE: __________

MERCHANDISE TOTAL	
SALES TAX	
POSTAGE	
INSURANCE	
TOTAL	

SIGNATURE: ______________________________

NOTE: CREDIT CARD MINIMUMS.

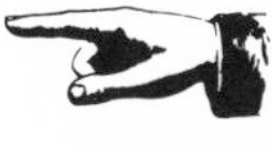

PAID WITH:

CREDIT CARD __________ CHECK __________ MONEY ORDER __________

PLEASE XEROX FOR ADDITIONAL ORDER FORMS.